CONCILIUM

Religion in the Eighties

CONCILIUM

Concilium 133 (3/1980): Dogma

THE RIGHT OF THE COMMUNITY TO A PRIEST

Edited by

Edward Schillebeeckx
and
Johann-Baptist Metz

English Language Editor
Marcus Lefébure

T. & T. CLARK LTD.
Edinburgh

THE SEABURY PRESS
New York

March 1980

T. & T. Clark Ltd., 36 George Street, Edinburgh EH2 2LQ
ISBN: 0 567 30013 7

The Seabury Press, 815 Second Avenue, New York, N.Y. 10017
ISBN: 0 8164 2275 3

Library of Congress Catalog Card No.: 80 50 477

Printed in Scotland by William Blackwood & Sons Ltd., Edinburgh

Concilium: Monthly except July and August.
Subscriptions 1980: All countries (except U.S.A. and Canada) £23·00 postage
and handling included; U.S.A. and Canada $54.00 postage and handling
included. (Second class postage licence pending at New York, N.Y.) Subscription
distribution in U.S. by Expediters of the Printed Word Ltd., 527 Madison
Avenue, Suite 1217, New York, N.Y. 10022.

CONTENTS

Part III
Theological Reflections

Part IV
Towards an Overall Evaluation

Editorial

MANY OF the faithful, including priests and bishops, appear to have short memories; for in their concrete reactions to the shortage of priests and in their proposals for a solution of this problem they evoke the traditional image of the priesthood. Everywhere we hear of new policy statements which have been inspired by that traditional image. Broadly speaking they follow these lines: in view of the growing shortage of priests, let us involve as many laypeople as possible in pastoral work (which by itself is indeed a plausible suggestion). In involving them let us even be loyal to them: let the lay persons do everything they are capable of in virtue of their expert knowledge of charism. But presiding at the Eucharist, at the service of reconciliation and at the sacramental service to the dying, in other words: the 'sacramental insertion' or 'ordinatio' is not for them. All this is reserved for those on whom the 'sacra potestas', the sacred power, is conferred at ordination as celibate candidates for the priesthood. This 'sacerdotium' or priesthood does not allow just any one, but only 'him'—a man—to share in a special way in the high priesthood of Christ, albeit somewhat less efficaciously for 'priests' than for those who possess episcopal power. In relation to the Christian community, the priest according to this vision is a *mediator between* Christ and the community. This sacerdotal mediation, which makes the ordained person 'another Christ', is based on a 'character' which the priest possesses, without any merit on his part, but nonetheless personally, in virtue of the equally sacred power of him who ordains him with the laying on of hands. As a result the priest possesses a power which he can exercise, unless the Church forbids him to do so, even on his own, without any member of the community being present. Moreover, this power cannot be lost; it is efficacious even, as Graham Greene puts it in one of his priest-novels: 'as an inoculation against small-pox'.

Let us be honest: this is roughly what we, the older generation, were still thinking about 20 years ago. Many of us even thought that this was a dogma of the Church. Even if it is not a Christian dogma, we must at least admit that the description just given is most certainly the official doctrine of the Latin-western Church. But we should add to this that this vision dates only from about the end of the twelfth century, which is fairly recent even as far as Latin Church history goes; and that it differs sensibly from conceptions of the ministry in the ancient Church. The medieval Ecumenical Councils unconsciously introduced a new conception and practice of the ecclesiastical ministry; in fact this was principally a new spirituality of the priesthood. What was experienced as almost a dogma in post-tridentine priestly spirituality is in fact nothing more than one determined concrete form of the ministry, very much historically conditioned. In view of the practice and thinking of the first Christian millennium, it could not possibly be something *unchangeable*. If this were the case it would imply that for ten centuries the Church was guilty of heretical practices or, reversely, that the ruling of Chalcedon about the ministry contained a direct condemnation of the Tridentine canons on the ministry. If this were the case the first and the second Christian millennium would be denying each other's Christian character.

Vis-à-vis the actually existing Church order we observe how many priests and lay people, moved by pastoral needs and by an evangelical concern for their fellow men, begin to develop an 'alternative' or parallel practice of building and guiding Christian communities; a practice which is directed less towards observance of laws than to the human person. They claim nevertheless to act according to the gospel of Jesus as the Christ.

This concrete pastoral situation explains the way this edition of *Concilium* has been planned and put together. In a first panoramic article an attempt is made to give a view of the total number of priests actually available to the Roman Catholic Church in the whole world (Jan Kerkhofs). In a second section the editors wished particularly to allow a number of actual experiences to speak for themselves. How do people in different regions react to the actual shortage of priests? What new ministerial practices are being developed? What are the concrete negative experiences resulting from a continued adherence to canon law?

We could naturally make only a selection out of what is in fact being done 'in the world', especially in many grass-roots or base communities, and in the official parishes-without-priests. The authors that have been approached come from Italy (G. Franzoni), Spain (J. Llopis), France (Monique Brulin), Holland (K. Derksen), North America (J. A. Komonchak) and finally South Africa (Fr. Lobinger). They have all in their own way answered the questions sent to them about their community's experiences. One author narrates what is in fact happening, legally or illegally, in many grass-roots communities. Other authors appear to assume as well-known the *de facto* 'non-conformist' usages and rather try to justify the 'exceptional' practices with the aid of pastoral or theological considerations. It is true that in this way part of the information escapes us, but it shows at the same time, that these 'new experiences' are not simply expressions of a 'wild' practice, but that they are the subject of theological reflection by the communities themselves.

All in all, however, the 'paradigmatic' facts are sufficiently numerous to allow of systematic reflection. This is done in a third section (S. Dianich; H. Waldenfels; N. Greinacher). That the present shortage of priests is also caused by historical blockages and decisions, like celibacy as a norm of admission to the ministry in the Latin-western Church, is analysed by H. J. Vogels. In this connection, celibacy is being studied simply as the 'paradigma' of an actual conflict between the apostolic right of a community to have a priest and prevailing Church legislation.

Finally we felt the need for a theological point of view which would synthesise the various aspects. How far can canonically illegal practices be theologically, pastorally and ethically justified? In what sense can 'new experiences' obtain normative force? In other words: How far can a new practice become a source of knowledge for dogmatic theology and its normative pronouncements?

As editors-in-chief of the Dogmatic Theology section we realise that both the experiences and the theological reflections in this edition will not make comfortable reading for the representatives and defenders of the ecclesiastical order actually in force. But we hope that they too will listen to the negative experiences of Church legislation which Christians have had, and by doing so become more sensitive to the damage being inflicted by present-day canon law on the forming of Christian communities, on the Eucharist, and on the ministry. The law of the Church which was formerly accepted as self-evident has in many respects now become a problem for many Christians. This edition is meant to be a contribution to a more sensitive formation of awareness with regard to the present problems of the ministry with which many Church communities are indeed struggling; problems that touch the very essence of the 'community of Christ'.

EDWARD SCHILLEBEECKX
JOHANN-BAPTIST METZ

Translated by B. J. Welling

PART I

*General Statistics about the
Situation of Priests*

Jan Kerkhofs

Priests and 'Parishes'—
A Statistical Survey

IT IS not without reason that the word 'parishes' appears between inverted commas. This article deals not only with what is canonically— and in general territorially—called a 'parish', but also takes into account, as far as possible, the many religious communities which form part of the organisational structure of the Church but which are not parishes or quasi-parishes in the strictest sense.

1. THE WORLD SITUATION

According to the *Annuarium Statisticum Ecclesiae—1976,*[1] in the whole of the world there were 129,810 parishes and quasi-parishes with a resident secular priest, 24,247 with a resident religious priest, and 44,157 without a permanent priest but served from elsewhere, in 1976. There were also 84 parishes entrusted to permanent deacons, 60 to male religious non-priests, 332 to nuns,[2] and 342 to lay people. There are 1,474 parishes, of which 1,129 are in Europe, with no one in charge. This last category covers some parishes which are nearly completely deserted, as often happens in France. Among the other categories there are parishes of enormous size with 40,000 or more faithful.

These figures should be supplemented by the number of mission posts on which many smaller communities or complete villages often depend. In 1976 there were 4,167 mission posts with a resident priest and 78,840 without a resident priest of which 38,138 were in Africa, 25,708 in Asia, 1,070 in Oceania and 8,626 in Latin America. From all this it follows that approximately half of all administrative Church units do not have a resident priest and that most social communities of the faithful have no priest in their midst.

A further analysis shows that the non-Western countries in particular are faced with a critical situation.

Parishes, quasi-parishes and mission posts with and without a resident priest[3]

	1	2	3	4	5
Africa	1,848	3,373	781	1,683	38,128
North America	18,574	3,477	1,590	398	3,602
Central America (Continent)	3,759	774	220	80	583
Central America (Antilles)	500	572	109	36	818
South America	8,223	4,960	1,720	196	8,626
America	31,056	9,783	3,639	710	13,629
Asia	6,523	2,825	1,322	1,454	25,708
Europe	88,840	7,682	40,502	149	305
Oceania	1,543	584	105	171	1,070
World total	129,810	24,247	46,349	4,167	78,840

1. Parishes and quasi-parishes with resident secular priest.
2. Parishes and quasi-parishes with resident religious priest.
3. Parishes and quasi-parishes without resident priest of which approximately 1,100 are without anyone having pastoral responsibility.
4. Mission posts with resident priest.
5. Mission posts without resident priest.

In the whole world there are 200,406 parishes and quasi-parishes, 83,007 mission posts, 44,465 'other pastoral centres', in all 327,878 official pastoral units. The average number of Catholics per unit is 2,210, varying from 820 in Africa to 9,060 on the continent of Central America.

By the end of 1976 there were in the whole world a total of 401,168 priests (of whom 241,379 were in Europe) divided into 256,573 seculars and 144,595 religious. There are on average 5·5 priests for every 10,000 Catholics, although the situation varies a great deal in the different regions, e.g., in North America 11·7, in Europe 9·2, in Africa 3·1 and in South America 1·6. These figures, however, do not disclose the big differences in the age pyramid, so that the real number of priests available for pastoral work is not known. Whereas the average age of secular priests about whom details are known is 43·6 years in Africa, this is 50·0 years in South America and 52·7 years in Europe (1976). Of the 243,307 secular priests whose age is known 46,126 are 65 years of age or older (of these 34,552 are in Europe) and 33,216 are under 35 years (19,324 of these are in Europe).

2. THE SITUATION IN SOME EUROPEAN COUNTRIES

There are numerous parishes in Western Europe without priests. The number is increasing rapidly and this will create a critical situation in many countries, particularly after 1985.

Parishes and quasi-parishes in Europe[4]

	With resident secular priest	With resident religious priest	Served by priest from other parish
Austria	2,053	592	394
Belgium	3,281	352	284
Czecho-Slovakia	2,642	224	1,259
France	15,597	832	20,851
DDR	732	47	117
Federal Republic	9,002	873	1,812
Italy	23,041	2,014	3,237
Netherlands	1,333	427	39
Poland	6,590	465	146
Portugal	2,612	117	1,593
Spain	12,133	696	8,543
Switzerland	1,338	149	191
Yugoslavia	1,831	372	475
Other countries	6,655	522	301
Total	88,840	7,682	39,242

Research conducted in France by the Centre National de Pastorale Liturgique (January 1977) showed that 1,100 parishes held Sunday worship without a priest (ADAP, assemblées dominicales en l'absence de prêtre).[5] Possibly this figure has increased by now to 1,700. These parishes are spread over 83 dioceses. This phenomenon started in 1967 and has grown continuously since then. At the same time the number of priests and of ordinations is forever decreasing.[6]

The situation is becoming rather serious also in some German dioceses. Whereas between 1950 and 1975 the number of priests in the Federal Republic and West Berlin fell from 14,600 to 11,423, the number of Catholics increased from 21·8 million to 28 million. First-year seminarists numbered 777 in 1962, fell to 312 in 1972 and increased again to 569 in 1977.

Compared with 504 ordinations in 1962, there were only 165 in 1977.[7] Pending the outcome of a national inquiry, some calculations in a few dioceses already indicate a somewhat general trend. According to forecasts, in 1984 there will be only 661 priests for pastoral care in the 1,025 parishes of the diocese of Rottenburg (2,112,000 Catholics). In the archdiocese of Freiburg i. Br. (2,361,000 Catholics) predictions are that in 1990 a maximum of 880 and a minimum of 657 priests will be available for 1,138 parishes. In Trier (1,958,000 Catholics) it is estimated that by 1985 only 343 priests will be engaged in pastoral work in approximately 1,000 parishes and quasi-parishes.[8] In 1965 there were 980 priests working in the 752 parishes of the archdiocese of München-Freising (2·2 million Catholics). In 1976 there were 770 and in 1984 they will probably have dwindled to 600.[9] The situation is more or less the same in the dioceses of Augsburg, Limburg, etc. The clergy is also ageing rapidly. In 1975 25 per cent of the priests in the diocese of Rottenburg was 65 years or older. In 1985 this figure will rise to 47 per cent and in 1995 to 65·5 per cent. The number of permanent deacons, however, is growing (120 in 1972, 467 in 1978), as is the number of lay theologians (*Laientheologen*) and pastoral assistants (*Pastoralassistenten*).

The number of parishes without a priest is also growing in Austria. According to F. Klostermann,[10] 30 of the 208 parishes in the northern region and 60 of the 269 parishes in the southern region of the diocese of Vienna were without a priest in 1977. It is expected that these figures will triple by 1988. A study by K. Pirker[11] reveals that in 1950, 32 of the 334 parishes in the diocese of Gurk-Klagenfurt were without a priest. In 1976 this figure had risen to 105 (31·4 per cent). Not only does the number of priests decrease, but their average age is also rising, and the burden of the pastoral care for each priest is becoming greater (one priest for 1,049 Catholics in 1945 compared with one priest for 1,620 Catholics in 1975).[12]

The following table is self-explanatory:

	1945	1975
Secular priests engaged in pastoral work	3,535	2,600
Religious priests engaged in pastoral work	1,127	1,118
Other secular priests in pastoral service	667	(603)
Total of priests engaged in pastoral work	5,329	4,321

K. Pirker notes that in the long run it will be impossible to replace the priests by lay people. A comparative study, concerning parishes with a resident priest and parishes which have been without a resident priest for any length of time, shows that not only do religious practices decline but in the latter case Christians are also much more prone to lapse. He establishes the following differences in the diocese of Karintia-Kärnten:

	Parishes with resident priest	Parishes without resident priest
Sunday observance	48%	30%
Easter duties	48%	32%
Communions per Catholic per year	11·0	3·0
Left the Church	5·2	7·8

In The Netherlands there are very few parishes without a priest. However, the same problems are looming also here. The number of priests and of ordinations to the priesthood is constantly decreasing and the average age of the clergy is rising fast. Whereas there were still 81 ordinations of secular priests in 1965, between 1975 and 1977 there were only 21, i.e., an average of 1 ordination per year and per diocese. At first, places which had become vacant could be occupied by religious priests,[13] but this source of supply is also drying up. In 1970 40 per cent of the parish clergy in the diocese of Groningen (101 parishes) came from religious orders and congregations, in 1979 this figure had increased to 63 per cent. Not one new secular priest has been ordained there since 1967. On the other hand the number of pastoral workers, both men and women, with higher theological qualifications and working full-time in the pastoral field, is continuously growing in The Netherlands, from 180 in 1977 to 236 in 1978.

Belgium, too, has very few parishes without a resident priest. But the number of priests is falling, the age pyramid is reversed in all dioceses and only 16 per cent of the vacant places, brought about by death and the increasing number of those leaving the priesthood, is occupied again by new ordinands. So far shortages have been made up by withdrawing priests from teaching and by recruiting religious priests. Before long this policy will come to an end. Between 1965 and 1975 the number of religious priests, in pastoral service of the archdiocese of Mechelen-Brussel, increased from 12·4 per cent to 27 per cent, and in 1978 to 33 per cent of the clergy engaged directly in pastoral care consisted of religious. If the present trend continues, a rise to 45 per cent in 1985 is expected. The total number of active priests has been falling by an average of 46 per year. The religious, too, have far less vocations than previously.

In 1978 there was only one new priest in the diocese of Antwerp (1,217,000 Catholics) who had been trained at the seminary. The number of active secular priests is constantly declining here also (1,074 in 1963, 954 in 1973, about 830 in 1978 and probably only 600 in 1988), and the number of religious working in the pastoral field has grown from 9 per cent in 1963 to 25 per cent in 1978. In 1978 the diocese of Antwerp covered 1,317 parishes in 33 per cent of which the parish priest was 60 years of age or older. There are as yet no parishes without a priest but some large parishes do not have a curate and soon more and more parishes will lose their resident priest.

B

The situation in the diocese of Basle in Switzerland is typical of the whole country, a few areas excepted. According to a study by Vicar-General A. Hopp,[14] it is estimated that there will be 530 secular and religious priests working in the diocese in 1985, compared with 758 in 1977 and 813 in 1970. In 1960 11·5 per cent and in 1977 31 per cent of the active clergy was older than 60 years. In the meantime the number of Catholics increased from 600,000 in 1950 to approximately 900,000 in 1970 (foreigners excepted). Whereas there was 1 priest for 964 Catholics in 1950, this figure will have risen to 1,700 in 1985. The number of parishes increased from 456 in 1950 to 526 in 1977. It is forecast that in 1985 there will be 325 priests available for 529 parishes, and in 1992 only 275 priests for the same number of parishes. In the beginning of 1977 there were 36 parishes without a resident priest (7 per cent), but very likely this figure will grow very rapidly. The number of lay theologians is increasing. From 84, of whom 4 were women, in 1977, the figure will probably rise to 120 in 1985 and to 150 in 1992. The number of teachers of religious instruction with a thorough theological training will very likely increase from 99 in 1977 (of them 65 were women of whom 17 were religious) to 140 in 1985 and 160 in 1992. If these predictions are correct, there will be 260 lay people in full-time service of the Church in 1985 and 310 in 1992 as compared with 530 and 425 priests respectively. Only very incomplete data are available for the rest of Europe, but evidently there are some areas in which the situation is even more precarious than in those mentioned above, e.g., in Portugal.

The situation in the diocese of Rome is entirely abnormal. Of the 293 parishes, covering 3·2 million people, 153 are served by religious and 140 by secular priests. The number of priests is falling and the average age is rising. The shortage-crisis of seminary students continues. There are only 23 students in the senior seminary of Rome, which means a maximum of 4 ordinations a year, proportionately less than those in The Netherlands.[15]

Even in England there is concern about the future. If the present trend continues, the number of active priests will fall from the present total of 3,800 to 2,200 within the next forty years.[16] A working party set up in Westminster diocese to study the reorganisation of the clergy (Working Group on the Redeployment of Clergy) proposed a number of recommendations which have been accepted by the bishops. Here, too, the average age is rising rapidly, and increasingly more large parishes are without a curate.[17]

3. THE UNITED STATES OF AMERICA AND CANADA

Many dioceses both in the United States and in Canada are very much in the same position. In Canada the number of priests has fallen rapidly and the average age of the clergy is rising considerably. In Quebec the average age of the secular priests is over 50 years. Of the religious priests 50 per cent will be older than 65 years in 1985. The religious no longer represent a sizeable source of supply to replace secular priests. In 1967 there were still 9,052 religious priests in Canada, in 1977 this figure had fallen to only 5,400. Several parishes have already been handed over to nuns. The number of priests active in a pastoral function in the United States decreased by 16 per cent (10,000 priests) between 1966 and 1978, the number of seminarists fell by 25,000. In 1978 there were only 13,960 as against 14,826 in 1977. In many dioceses the average age of the clergy is rising rapidly, even though the number of vocations is growing again in some dioceses and in some religious congregations.

It should be realised, however, that 25 per cent of American Catholics speak Spanish and that there are 300 Spanish-speaking American priests and about 1,000 priests from Spain or Latin America for more than 12 million Catholics. A similar situation is encountered among the black Catholic population, e.g., in Detroit there is 1 black priest for 30,000 black Catholics.

4. OTHER CONTINENTS

Detailed studies as to the numbers of priests in relation to the religious communities in other continents show a picture that completely differs from that in the West. Some examples will illustrate this. Apart from about 80 indigenous and 200 foreign priests there are more than 4,000 'lideres de comunidades' in Honduras who bear the main responsibility for the local communities. In the Dominican Republic (approximately 5 million people, only 130 indigenous priests—even after five centuries of Catholicism—and about 500 foreign priests) there are a great number of 'community chairmen'. In the diocese of Santiago de los Caballeros alone there are already 500. They act, in fact, as the 'pastores' of the 'priestless' communities.[18] Similar situations are to be found in Peru,[19] Bolivia, large regions of Brazil, Mexico, etc.

Taking Latin America as a whole, in 1974 there was 1 priest for 6,160 Catholics as compared with 1 for every 4,985 in 1969. In Brazil the proportion is even 1 to 8,546. Between 1965 and 1975 the overall number of priests fell in various countries, such as Argentina, Chile, Ecuador, Nicaragua, Peru. But even in those countries, where the absolute figure increased, the ratio between priests and population decreased, e.g., in Mexico, a Latin American country that, after Brazil, has the highest number of priests, the number of priests increased from 7,293 in 1965 to 9,093 in 1975, but the ratio fell from 1 priest to 5,514 people in 1970 to 1 priest to 6,648 people in 1976. At the same time the number of seminary students is decreasing:[20]

Senior seminary students	1969	1976
Seculars	2,687	1,925
Religious	944	575
Total	3,631	2,500

Mexico has a population of more than 66 million (1979) which is expected to grow to more than 120 million by the year 2000. It should also be remembered that in many South American countries most priests are religious and many are foreigners. It is impossible to give a sufficiently detailed picture of the situation in Asia and Africa within the scope of this article. The number of baptised people is rising much faster than that of priests. The foreign clergy in Africa is becoming older and is not proportionately replaced by indigenous priests. There are many local communities in Asia, even in India, without a priest. The situation is so serious that the Indian Pastoral Conference (Bangalore 1976) as well as the Colloquium on the Ministry, organised by the Federation of Asian Bishops' Conferences (FABC) (Hong Kong 1977),[21] pointed out the great need of many areas and requested new solutions.

CONCLUSION

Large areas of the Church seem to have arrived at an impasse, because the number of priests is disproportionate to the number of communities. In some countries this situation has gone on for generations, sometimes centuries. Yet, in the early centuries of the Church, and also during many centuries afterwards, there was a normal ratio of 1 priest to every 50 to 300 faithful.

Translated by W. M. P. Kruyssen

Notes

1. Secretaria Status (Rome 1978), pp. 59-118.
2. Of these 39 are in Africa, 23 in North America, 224 in Central and South America, 17 in Asia and 29 in Europe.
3. *Annuarium Statisticum Ecclesiae—1976,* l.c.
4. *ibid.*
5. M. Brulin 'Assemblées dominicales en l'absence de prêtres; situation en France et enjeux pastoraux' *La Maison-Dieu* 130 (2/1976) 80-113.

6. From a peak of 646 in 1965 to 99 in 1977. 1978 saw an increase (118) but this was exceptional in view of the numbers of seminary students in the next few years.

7. In 1975 there were 170 ordinations but, on the other hand, 436 priests died and 36 left the ministry. Even if the present upward trend continues, there will still be a great shortage of priests over the next 20 years or more.

8. N. Greinacher 'Das Problem der nichtordinierten Bezugspersonen in katholischen Gemeinden' *Diakonia* (Sept. 1978) 404-412.

9. F. Klostermann *Wir brauchen Priester* (Linz 1977).

10. *ibid.*

11. Quoted by P. M. Zulehner *Wie kommen wir aus der Krise? Kirchliche Statistik Oesterreichs 1945-1975 und ihre pastoralen Konzequenzen* (Vienna 1978) p. 34.

12. The number of lay people working full-time in the pastoral field is also rising in Austria, e.g., in the three dioceses of St Pölten, Feldkirch and Linz from 69 in 1945 to 416 in 1975.

13. In the whole of The Netherlands there were, in 1977, 900 religious priests in charge of 455 parishes and 43 quasi-parishes. Added to this, approximately another 750 religious priests were working in parishes of which seculars were in charge.

14. Bistum Basel *Personalprognose, Fragmente eines Pastoralkonzeptes* (1978). According to the study *Bistum St Gallen 1990* the expectations for 1990 were 151 priests as against 196 in 1978. A new assessment now puts the latter figure at 95-100.

15. In Italy the numerical ratio between priests and people is becoming increasingly worse. Between 1961 and 1977 the population increased from 50·6 million to 56·6 million, the number of parishes grew from 25,919 to 28,071, but the secular clergy fell from 43,538 to 40,886. At the same time the number of ordinations to the priesthood (seculars) declined from a peak of 918 in 1966 to a new low of 384 in 1978. Between 1961 and 1978 the total number of seminary students both in senior and junior seminaries fell from 29,982 to 9,853 and is still falling. In 1961 there were 3,673 theology students, in 1978 only 1,634—see A. Nicora 'Seminari e vocazioni oggi in Italia' *Il Regno—Documenti* (Bologna), 11/79, 283-284, and see also 291-293.

16. These figures have been added from statistics recently published (translator's note).

17. *The Tablet* (London), 22/7/78, p. 714.

18. *La República Dominicana y su pastoral, PMV Informes, América Latina* (Brussels) 13/1978 pp. 41-44.

19. *L'Eglise au sein des peuples indigènes d'Amérique latine* PMV Bulletin 52/1974 pp. 30-31.

20. *Ministros y ministerios en América Latina, PMV Informes, América Latina* (Brussel) 6/1977.

21. *Ministries in the Church in India,* Research Seminar and Pastoral Consultation ed. D. S. Amalorpavadass (Bangalore) 1976; FABC, *Asian Colloquium on Ministries in the Church* ed. P. de Achutegui (Hong Kong) 1977 pp. 32-34, 48-50.

PART II

Accounts of Lived Experiences

Giovanni Franzoni

An Account of Experiences in Italy

1. THE CLASS OPTION

CHRONOLOGICALLY speaking, the problem of ministries was not the first with which basic ecclesial community in Italy had to deal. Groups, communities and parishes sought above all some form of identification with the condition of the oppressed and marginalised, in order to attempt a rereading of the Christian faith from the point of view of the latter. Using current terminology, though without claiming to make an automatic transposition of the Marxist concept, people spoke in terms of the 'class option'.

Since the links which the institutional Church established in the course of history with the economic, political and ideological power of the ruling classes constituted a form of conditioning, the first spontaneous impulse was to break free from this situation.

It Italy, the Vatican's link with those in power revolved in the main round two centres. First and foremost, the Concordat between Church and State, which was drawn up in 1929 and confers on the Church a number of privileges, ascribing to it a precise role in the process of acquiring the consent of the masses to the established order. And secondly, Christian Democracy as the political expression of the cultural hegemony of the Italian Church and an instrument of the exercise of power.

In certain situations in the South, one could mention in addition the Mafia, a powerful criminal organisation, particularly active in Sicily and in Calabria, inexorably cutting off every voice of dissent and of rebellion against those in power, an instrument used knowingly on occasion by the Christian Democrats, to which the local Church has been unable to adopt any attitude but that of resignation.

15

If the basic communities are fundamentally committed to breaking free from these centres of power and have sometimes, to this end, highlighted the leadership and indeed the sacral role of the ordained priest, this should not be interpreted as disregard for the biblical evidence or as theological under-development, but rather as a consequence of the fact that renewal in the Church does not only take place in the realm of theoretical reflection, but comes up against and is set in motion by concrete social and political conditions.

2. REAPPROPRIATION OF THE WORD AND OF THE ECCLESIAL STRUCTURES

In order that this experience of freeing the Church from its relationship with the power structure should be a true ecclesial experience and not simply a political struggle, it was essential that an immediate and ecclesial reading of the Bible should be made possible once more. The Bible was known to Italian Catholics almost exclusively through the filter of the magisterium—a magisterium which placed itself *above* the Church and *between* the Church and the Word of God, instead of serving the Word *within* the Church.

Mediated in this heavy-handed way, the biblical texts, and in particular the Gospel, reach the ecclesial community in a truncated state, isolated from their context and, what is more, *presented* in sermons that are far more concerned to pass on the concept of obedience than the prophetic message.

It is worth noting the documentary evidence gathered by the basic community of Alghero (Sassari). In *L'ha detto il parroco* (Ora Sesta, Milan, 1975) it brought together a number of sermons that had been preached in various churches in the city, demonstrating that what was being put across was not the announcement of the saving act of Christ but rather a moralistic and spiritualistic message for purely individual consumption.

If the historical basis for this rereading of the Bible was the struggle of the oppressed, the exegetical tools were provided by those who already possessed them beforehand. Here too the ordained priest who had followed a special course of study became a functional element in the reappropriation by the community of the Word of God.

The concept of reappropriation does not absolutely exclude the service of the bishop, but it calls on the bishops to exercise their ministry *within* the community and not *from above*. To take renewed possession of the Bible and the sacraments does not imply inventing them from scratch but treating them as 'God's gift to the Church as a whole'.

This rereading of the gospel has also led to a different use of the ecclesial structures. By structures can be understood both the parish buildings and the Church itself seen as a sacred place, and certain functions of the priest within the context of the social and health services, religious education and so on.

A choice of this kind—indispensable if one was to be saved from mere intellectual research and instead place at the disposal of the oppressed in their struggles those structures which have always been used to exploit them—involved entering an area in which, thanks to the Italian Concordat, the hierarchy would always be the strongest. It is in fact enough that the diocesan curia should withdraw its *nihil obstat* and a chaplain or professor of religion will lose his post automatically. And whenever church buildings have been used to shelter gatherings of striking workers (as for example in the case of the workers of La Vingone in the Church at Isolotto), the reaction of the bishops has invariably been to insist on the sacred character of the building, accusing the priests of putting it to political use and of no longer being 'above parties' in wilful ignorance, of course, of the fact that throughout the centuries the sacred building and the parish structure in general in all its aspects (from the baptismal register to the cemetry) was always a centre of social and political control; and ignoring too the fact that, although nominally neutral, the priest in Italy was always, implicitly or explicitly, a supporter of the Christian Democrats, and therefore had always *engaged in politics* by making use of ecclesial structures like the pulpit and the confessional.

3. REAPPROPRIATION OF THE ORDAINED PRIEST

The Italian hierarchy responded to the 'profane' use of ecclesial structures and juridically sanctioned roles by imposing restraint where it was able to do so: on the priest as representative of the bishop. Whence the withdrawal of the *mandate* or *nihil obstat* from chaplains and professors of religion, and the removal of parish priests or curates (and sometimes even of bishops) for 'pastoral' reasons.

The most significant examples of this were those that occurred in parishes where the people responded to the removal of their parish priest by aligning themselves solidly round the minister whose role they *recognised* henceforward from below.

Whenever a parish priest was removed for having publicly adopted positions that diverge from the line presupposed by the Concordat (at Oregina, near Genoa, in 1971, a marriage was celebrated in which the civil rite was separated from the religious rite; at Isolotto, near Florence, solidarity was expressed with those who were occupying the Cathedral in Parma), the community's response was to invite the bishop to come and talk to everyone and not to deal with the parish priest in isolation as if he were his steward. Then in 1973 such cases multiplied in conjunction with the referendum on divorce, when, contrary to the line laid down by the bishops, many priests declared themselves in favour of the freedom of Catholics to vote according to their own consciences. Many communities, whose relationship with the hierarchy was already tense, either because their preaching was regarded as too progressive or because of their political positions, were struck by the removal of their parish priest or with the suspension of their priests *a divinis*. Some communities (Isolotto, Lavello, Gioiosa, Jonica) occupied the church premises, and were subsequently confronted with long and costly legal processes. Others, like the community of S. Paolo in Rome or that of S. Anna in Gorizia, preferred to move themselves bodily to another location and there continue to celebrate the Eucharist and the sacraments of baptism and matrimony in a situation tolerated by those in authority.

In certain cases the Eucharist is celebrated out in the open in the *piazza* (Isolotto, Oregina, San Pietro in Sala, Milan), or else a public building is found in which to call together the assembly of the Lord.

The common factor in all these cases is the obvious antagonism that exists between the *recognition* of the ministry by the hierarchy and its recognition by the community. In their reflections on the matter, basic communities certainly do not deny that the grace and the ministers come from God; they are seen, however, as gifts made by the Spirit to the Church, not to the bishops.

Reducing the matter to its simplest terms, one might say that, as the Italian bishops see things, God gives the bishops the power to transmit both the grace and the ministries to the people; according to the mind of the people of the community, the Lord gives the grace and the Gospel to the People of God and the latter creates for itself the historical forms which the ministries and the sacraments take. It is quite clear that the point at issue, which needs to be reflected on and discussed by theologians, is the claim that an investiture took place once and for all among the apostles and has since been transmitted by dynastic succession or the imposition of hands.

One final observation. In almost all these cases, the basic communities did not respond to the removal or suspension *a divinis* of their priest by putting a layman in his place or confiding the presidency of the Eucharist to lay people, but by opposing the decision taken by the bishop in an administrative manner and calling on him to do so before the people. The first time that the Oregina community celebrated the Eucharist without the bishop's permission, with 17 priests from various places, it left out the proclamation of the Word as a sign of penitence for the absence of the bishop. Apart from Fr. Michele Pellegrino, Archbishop of Turin, who took part in an assembly of the community of Vandalino, and Don

Clemente Riva, Auxiliary Bishop of southern Rome, and a few others, the bishops have as a rule responded to the communities' invitation by invoking their own authority and recognising only those priests who agreed to be the representatives of authority among the people.

4. COMMUNITY AND EUCHARIST

Alongside this experiment in the reappropriation of the 'ordained priesthood', yet another original experiment is emerging, that of those communities who are living the Eucharist and the proclamation of the Word without the *presidency* of an ordained priest.

The community of Peretola and that of the Resurrection in Florence, both of them related to the faith experience of Don Luigi Rosadoni, reached the decision, after his death in 1972, to celebrate the Eucharist even when there was no ordained priest present. This practice has become the norm in these two communities, but others too, such as that of Isolotto in Florence or of S. Anna in Gorizia, while they ordinarily left the role of president at the Eucharist to an ordained priest, nevertheless went ahead with the celebration of Mass in the absence of one.

At the seminar on ministries, which took place in Rome in September 1974, the community of Peretola summed up its own development as follows: 'When we left the parish, there was no priest in our group, but we celebrated the Eucharist with various priests whom we knew. . . . Subsequently, for contingent reasons, which we summarise not in order to establish a theory of ecclesial ministry, but in order to define certain stages of a particular experiment, we gradually came to the point, as the community matured, of doing without the priest. . . . After a number of weeks without the Eucharist we considered that the validity of the Eucharistic sign should be and was linked to the prophetic position of the community, to its straining towards a certain type of proclamation and experience as well as towards a particular type of struggle; it was argued that when this tension is realised in the community, then and only then does *the body and blood* of Christ become a present reality. . . . Given that no priest emerged from among ourselves and that, even had there been one, unless he found himself to be in communion with us, the Eucharistic sign, which had value as an expression of faith and hope, would have lost its meaning and become trivialised . . . we no longer succeeded in according the Eucharist its value as a grace from above. Throughout the history of the Church the People of God have delegated to a priest the task of celebrating the Eucharist as a sign of unity, and this in effect has been a service rendered by the priest. It seemed to us essential in our situation that we should regain possession of this faculty . . . and since then we have celebrated the Eucharist among ourselves, with the scriptural readings, the prayers of the rite and so on. We do not theorise, however, as to which priestly ministry is authentic; indeed, if a priest happens to be present we readily invite him to preside at the Eucharist. . . . We simply say that this is something that has happened in our community in the course of its development for reasons which seem valid to us and in which we believe; but for obvious reasons we are not trying to put forward any kind of model.'

5. THE SEMINAR: 'ECCLESIAL COMMUNION AND MINISTRIES IN THE CHURCH'

Even from the methodological point of view, this seminar, which took place in Rome in September 1974, stands out as a significant event. In the course of it in fact, apart from the reports of the communities and the contributions of individual lay people, the collaboration of theologians was called for. In his introductory address Filippo Gentiloni, of the community of S. Paolo, said: 'We are convinced that the *place* for theology is the basic community which reflects on its own experience of faith in the light of the Word of God. Obviously we are not setting out to formulate a new theology to place alongside or substitute for earlier theologies. We simply maintain that you can only elaborate a theology in the appropriate surroundings, those of a community of faith which exists in the perspective of the gospel, that is on the side of the poor, the exploited and the oppressed—or in other words, to use current terminology, in the perspective of the class option. In this way we sought to recover and, by putting it in its historical context, to define more precisely, that *sensus fidelium* of which classical theology has always spoken.'

From the final report there emerged a theology of priesthood and ministries which could at some future date incorporate experiments like those of the communities of La Peretola and the Resurrection, while at the same time trying not to break with the overall process of renewal in the universal Church. 'It is for the community as such', states the final document, 'to be the subject of the ministries which emerge from the community for the service of mankind. Attention must therefore be shifted from the ministry of the individual priest to the multiplicity of ministries which should be carried on within the community. Even at the risk of coming into conflict with the existing ecclesiastical authorities, it is necessary to "immerse" the ministries in the general context of the community in such a way as to abolish the priestly caste by neutralising its authority. . . .' The communities wish to remain faithful to the principle according to which the only priest of the New Covenant is Christ, in whose priesthood all the faithful participate. It is necessary therefore to place in its true perspective the role of the priest, which is often founded on scriptural testimony taken from the Old rather than from the New Testament.'

6. THE LATEST DEVELOPMENTS

The marriage of Rosario Mocciaro, one of the priests of the community of San Paolo (the civil ceremony in the municipality, the religious in the community) and his consequent reduction to the lay state by the authorities posed once again for the community of San Paolo the problem of who was to preside at the Eucharist.

On this occasion too, to the breach which would have been caused had a layman been invited to preside at the Eucharist and which could have been interpreted, albeit wrongly, as a breach at the doctrinal level, a breach at the disciplinary level was preferred.

Finding a number of non-celibate priests available, therefore, the community invited them to preside, on the clear understanding that the community is the celebrating subject (in the community, the canon of the Mass is recited in unison).

Thus the various positions that are to be found within the community of San Paolo reflect fairly well the general picture in Italy as a whole. (a) Priests who preside at the Eucharist, with various qualifications accepting their role, and who are tolerated by the bishop. (b) Priests who preside at the Eucharist and accept the ministry with the same qualifications, but who have broken with the authorities at the disciplinary level. (c) Priests who, like the present writer, although they accept the ministry, do not preside at the Eucharist because they have been involuntarily reduced to the lay state. This *disobedient obedience* has worked wonders in some of them. It is not based merely on expediency, nor is it simply the result of personal hesitancy. It is rooted in the conviction that every religious sign remains ambiguous in the last analysis, and that one would be wrong to allow it to become a source of conflict between the basic community and the hierarchy, whether on theological questions or on the option in favour of the poor. (d) Priests who do not preside at the Eucharist because they radically reject every ministerial role. Some of these asked for a dispensation when the moment came, but others deny or reject completely the competence of the ecclesiastical authorities and live their lives of faith and their political commitment fully as laymen.

As far as further reading is concerned, reference may be made to a full and reasoned bibliography on 'basic communities and ecclesial ministries' edited by Pier Giorgio Paterlini and published in Com/Nuovi Tempi (August 1978).

Translated by Sarah Fawcett

Joan Llopis

Accounts of Experiences in Spain

I CONSULTED a young layman belonging to a small Christian community in a densely populated Spanish city on the general theme of this issue of *Concilium,* and he produced the following written reflections, which indicate the precise dimensions of the problem, and present a living experience which is a typical example of it. He writes:—

'Undoubtedly the decline in the numbers of available clergy which we are experiencing in our country at present produces negative repercussions, especially in the territorial organisation of the Church: parishes without a priest, etc. But it also produces positive results: it obliges us at last, at the practical level, to face up to a whole series of problems which were being shelved. Such, for example, as the whole question of the organisation of ministries within the Christian community.

'Clearly it is easier to raise the question in that part of the Church which is usually described by such expressions as "evangelistic movements", and which is composed of Christians who are more active in their faith, more highly organised, and who find it easier to adapt themselves to new situations such as those resulting from the shortage of clergy. But that does not make the experience of such sectors of the Church any less valid, and indeed we can draw from it elements which are useful for the whole Church.

'Up to now, these movements themselves have depended very much on the priests, through the well-known figure of the "counsellor". Each group, however small it might be, had a counsellor, who guided it in the right way and celebrated mass when necessary. But this is coming to an end. Today it is already Utopian to suppose that every little meeting of

22

seven or eight people can count on one of these men, trained in the seminaries, ordained by a bishop, and, like good civil servants, directed in their movements and tasks by the ecclesiastical establishment.

'What can be done then? We could eliminate the small groups and establish only as many groups as there were priests available. Or we could cease to celebrate the Eucharist within these communities. Unsatisfactory solutions. How can the word of the gospel reach each individual person except through the small group? And how can a group express its faith unless its members share together the bread and wine of Jesus Christ?

'The problem is a real and living one. I know of many groups which are tackling it, and in fact I belong to one of them. I know of some groups which cannot see their way clear to celebrate the Eucharist without a priest. It is a difficult step to take. In my group too there were doubts— felt as real, rather than formulated in words. No one was able to see clearly (or at any rate "very clearly") why the Eucharist should not be celebrated without a priest, but it was a step that was hard to take. We tried it out, and at first found it difficult. There was a certain uncomfortableness, a certain hesitancy, arising not simply from the question of the presence or absence of the priest, but from doubts about "how it should be done", or "what needed to be done" so that it might be "truly" a Eucharist.

'Undoubtedly it was as a result, more of less unconscious, of this initial difficulty in overcoming the kind of obstacle we encounter in this field, that after our earlier experiences we continued to meet for a time without celebrating the Eucharist. It has to be remembered that the tradition of the group was for fairly elaborate celebrations, with readings, hymns, creeds, vestments, flowers, candles, etc. Long celebrations, with a considerable degree of solemnity, at least for a small group. And celebrations in which the priest played a central role. That too helped to make the impact of what we were doing greater, and in fact we remained for a time unable to take the decision to celebrate together.

'But the need was there. It is difficult to maintain a believing community, however small it may be, without sharing together the sign which binds us to Jesus Christ and the Church. And so we have resumed our celebrations of the Eucharist. At an extremely simple level. Seven or eight people, in the little living rooms of some of those small apartments which they are building these days. The reading of the gospel, and, perhaps, of a poem or passage which may have appealed to someone. Comment on the texts, or on whatever the person concerned wishes. In the centre, from the start, a little low table with bread and wine. Bread from the bakery, and wine from the inn. Nothing more. Except a little music to accompany the silences and to give a little atmosphere to the occasion, music chosen more or less at random, within certain limits, from the recordings that are available today. At the appropriate moment we remember the action of Jesus at the Last Supper, reading the account from one of the gospels or from Paul. And we share the bread and the wine. And that is all.

'What will happen in the future? Shall we gradually enrich the celebration by adding more elements to it? Shall we include hymns? Or flowers? Or creeds? We shall have to wait and see. But what we have certainly experienced is that the celebration retains all its power, all its significance, however simple its outward form may be. What we will not tolerate is to be told that we must not celebrate the Eucharist. This we believe firmly: Jesus Christ is alive for us, and the community share his body and his blood, his full reality.

'Very well then. We are talking about a particular case, about an experience. Perhaps it is not something that can be applied generally. It is true that we who belong to the group are people with much Christian history behind us, involved in Church activities, in constant contact with other believers, with theological books, with Christian reviews, with religious orders, with priests. It could easily be said that although priests are absent from the group they are all the time looking in from just outside. That is probably true. But we do not regard ourselves as an exceptional group; we believe that there can be many groups like ours, and indeed we know that they exist. We are agreed that this "external" contact with the Church is good and indeed indispensable. But that does not detract from our experience nor from what we are trying to say now.

'Perhaps the situation is not ideal? Again, we would agree. But I do not believe that the situation would be any more ideal if once again many more people were to receive "vocations", and if each group could go back to having its own "seminary priest". What we have to do, the way we have to profit from the present situation, is to take the opportunity of raising again the whole question of ministries in the community. The ideal at which we have to aim is to see what needs to be done to safeguard the life of Christian communities. Will it be necessary for someone in each group to take responsibility for preparing the celebrations? Clearly it will. And that there should be someone who presides over them? Certainly. That these should be temporary responsibilities? Obviously. That the allocation of responsibilities should be given some sort of liturgical expression? I think so. That someone in the community should be responsible for maintaining contact with other communities for their mutual enrichment? Very clearly. That it would be good for someone to review the progress of the community with some other person, priest or otherwise, who could help to keep it on the right lines? Yes, that would be good. But so long as we are not progressing towards this ideal we cannot stand with arms folded. The bishop is not going to make these changes for us overnight. We ourselves will have to set about doing them, slowly. And while we are doing them, and, indeed, so that we may do them successfuly, we must keep our communities alive and active, and within them we must continue to celebrate the Eucharist, the great sign of our faith in Jesus Christ.'

It is difficult to know exactly how many groups there are in our country of the kind reflected in the foregoing experience, but, whether they are few or many, they present a very serious challenge to theological reflection. I know of a down-town community which, finding itself left without a priest, continued to celebrate the Eucharist without any priest presiding. The person responsible for the pastoral oversight of the area told them that while what they were doing was a celebration religiously valid for them, the theologians would tell them that it was not a proper Eucharist. Nevertheless, the members of this community, like the young men in the foregoing narrative, are firmly convinced that they are celebrating the living memorial of Jesus Christ. Recently the community has been joined by a priest, who, it appears, so as not to cause offence, is to be charged with the celebration of the Eucharist, although the meeting will continue to be presided over by a layman—a situation which poses an even more serious theological problem: the dichotomy between the function of presiding over the assembly and that of 'administering' the sacrament.

More common are the cases where a community dispenses with the services of a priest for the celebration of other sacraments, like marriage for example. If two members of the community wish to marry, once they have gone through the legal formalities and the civil ceremony, they meet with the members of their faith-community and express before them their desire to be united to each other in Christ: so far as they are concerned this is enough to make their marriage Christian, without any necessity for the canonical intervention of the Church or the blessing of a priest.

Up to now I have been mentioning experiences in which it can be clearly seen that the initiative comes from the community itself. Its members see themselves deprived of the presence of a priest and then, in a manner more or less thought out, come to the practical conclusion that they can—and indeed must—perform those signs which are of the essence of the Christian faith without the presence of an ordained minister. My personal impression is that none of these cases is yet very common in Spain, although in the long run they may act as a ferment and have unexpectedly wide repercussions.

Much more common—though even these are not yet a large-scale phenomenon—are the cases where the initiative comes from the side of the priests. Many diverse examples could be given of priests whose personal experience leads them to abandon the existing ecclesiastical system and seek new ways of exercising their ministry. Some end up leaving the ministry, but others do not consider this necessary and, though they are almost always misunderstood by the official bodies, try to rediscover a pattern of sacerdotal activity in which their evangelistic presence in the midst of life is more important than performing sacramental functions *ex officio*.

In this sense, the experience of a Catalan priest, who died recently while still relatively young, is very significant. He felt obliged to abandon the traditional practice of ministry, centred on the administration of the sacraments, so as to be able to make contact with the inhospitable reality of the working-class district in which his parish was situated. His missionary vocation led him to want to share completely the life of the people of his district, and, in consequence, to exercise a ministry shorn of all rites and signs, letting it be simply a human presence sustained by his radical faith in Jesus Christ. He came to renounce completely the ritual sacraments, because he saw them as devoid of the reality which they were supposed to signify and celebrate, and he himself died without sacraments, although his death, after a painful illness, was a most eloquent sign of his faith and of his love.

Another significant case is that of a priest of mature years who, after having been intensely active in parochial life and in the field of specialised movements, cut himself off from the institutional Church, and, later, left the ministry and married, motivated by the desire to rid himself of every kind of clerical 'power'.

We will allow the man to state his own case:—

'The priest has "power" over the most intimate part of man—his conscience. He is the one who transmits doctrinal and normative orthodoxy. This is so even though the priest himself may not want it. As a first step, I discuss this question with a study group. In the meantime I go on exercising my ministry. My "power" is for people's good, but it is "power" when all is said and done. This power which is used for the good of others is called "service" by many. But it does not permit people to grow and mature. The prevailing idea is always that of the "shepherd and his sheep". I and the others: I, who in the name of God lead them to green pastures, and they who, like obedient and submissive sheep, come after me. For this reason there comes a day when I leave the ministry. So far as the institution is concerned, I am still a priest. In my own view, I am one no longer. Without the ministry, priesthood has no meaning. Later, after a few years, I get married.'

We have to recognise that the foregoing case is not concerned simply with the story of an individual, but that other priests and all the members of a Christian community are involved in it. Let us take a look at the way the community developed:—

'We begin, with quite a large group of persons, to form the community. The priest acts as priest: he celebrates the Eucharist, baptises, etc. We priests do not want to be different from the other members, and we identify ourselves more and more as time goes on with the laymen (in work, in politics, etc.). We do it, and we say it often. But there is no getting away from our cultural conditioning, or from the deep-rooted conscience of the laymen. In their view, we are like them, but with something more. Then the group is reduced. The priest continues to act as priest, but we celebrate the Eucharist jointly (common reading of the anaphora). We leave the parish ministry and we live out our faith with the community through the Eucharist and prayer. Now the priest no longer acts as priest. All this is not achieved in a single day, in view of the sociological and cultural weight which attaches to the role of the priest in the believers' life of faith. For us, all that matters is the community, our companions. We live out our lives in common, we pray together and we celebrate the Eucharist. None is greater than any other and we are all believers. We are open to all those people who, liberated or in the process of being liberated from burdens and restrictions, live out or try to live out their faith in God and in Jesus with a human life that is "seriously lived".'

There are also experiences similar to the foregoing, in which the community asks the secularised priest to continue to preside over its Eucharists. Although all consider themselves equal, there remains the conviction that if there is to be someone who leads the meeting it is better that the person who is technically best prepared for it should do it.

It would be a mistake to think that all the experiences there have been in this area of the quest for new ways of exercising ministry are the result of initiatives by the basic communities or by more or less restless priests. The problem also preoccupies the hierarchical authorities, who have urged the promotion of lay ministries and have established norms for the setting up of the permanent diaconate, without however, producing very many practical results. A rural diocese has organised a regular pastoral service and entrusted it to nuns, who on Sundays are responsible for presiding over celebrations of the Word and for distributing communion in villages which have no priest and can only take advantage of the celebration of the Eucharist at infrequent intervals. It is interesting to observe that the people speak of the 'nun's mass', from which it may be supposed that simple village people would have little difficulty in admitting that the Eucharist could indeed be celebrated by someone who was not a priest.

Be that as it may, the experiences we have related—and we do not claim that they are either exhaustive or complete—show that in Spain, as in other countries in the Catholic world, a very interesting movement is growing up which is trying to find ways of solving what has been called the crisis of identity of the priesthood—which, fundamentally, is also a crisis of identity for the Christian community. It is a movement which must be submitted to the judgment of theology, but which must not under any circumstances be condemned in advance.

Translated by G. W. S. Knowles

Monique Brulin

Sunday Assemblies Without a Priest in France: Present Facts and Future Questions

OVER THE last ten years, documents of different kinds and from varying sources—articles in local or national newspapers; gossip columns; review articles in the Catholic press; papers collected or published by parishes, dioceses and national Catholic organisations—have been reporting the existence of 'Sunday assemblies', that is, of meetings of Catholic Christians which take place on a Sunday, without a priest, at the places and times usual for Sunday mass.

The institutional Church seems to have started taking a systematic interest in these assemblies in 1971. In that year, the National Centre for Pastoral Liturgy conducted a survey of the diocesan liturgical commissions in order to review what they were doing and how they were contributing to the pastoral effort of the French Church as a whole. Among other developments considered to be new, the survey revealed the occurrence of 'liturgical services held without a priest, particularly on Sundays'.

It is these services that we shall be discussing here. After a general account of the position today, we shall endeavour to analyse how the movement came into existence. We shall then try to show how it may be affecting the traditional view of roles and responsibilities, and how, finally, though it is limited in scope, it is raising fundamental questions about the way Christian communities are organised.

1. SUNDAY ASSEMBLIES: A GENERAL PICTURE

1. *The situation in France*

In January 1977, the National Centre for Pastoral Liturgy held a further survey of the dioceses; this section of our article is largely based

29

on the results then obtained. Clearly, information collected through such channels must reflect the view of Church officials, and the figures given in the replies doubtless fall short of the reality. In all probability, however, they are sufficiently accurate to form the basis of a nationwide picture of the situation.[1]

Of the 92 dioceses in France, 67 mention regular Sunday assemblies without a priest. 725 parishes are involved, in 484 of which the meetings are held in a number of different places, on a rota system. If the less regular assemblies are included too, about 1,200 parishes are involved, though this figure is almost certainly too low. 80 per cent or so of these parishes are in localities with under 1,000 inhabitants; 50 per cent in localities with under 500 inhabitants.

The movement seems to have begun in 1967, in the diocese of le Mans. However, few diocesan reports mention it before 1973, when a document by the plenary assembly of French bishops, '*Tous responsables dans l'Eglise?*', was published, and had a strong influence on what was decided in some dioceses.[2] From 1973 to 1975 the number of assemblies increased rapidly. It then levelled off, but is still gradually rising.

The frequency with which assemblies meet varies between two to four times a year at one extreme, and every Sunday at the other. The weekly meetings, which are relatively uncommon, are to be found in villages that are becoming depopulated and are difficult to reach; these villages have mass on a weekday and on a few special feasts during the year. By contrast, in 38·6 per cent of the parishes concerned, the assembly is held on one Sunday a month; in 32 per cent, on two Sundays a month, and in 4·8 per cent, on three Sundays a month.

The numbers of people present at the services range from 10 to 300, and are very close to those for mass, although seemingly slightly lower. At more than half the assemblies, the congregation numbers between 15 and 50.

There is usually more than one person or team concerned with organising the services; in many cases, this was a prerequisite for the assembly to be set up. Almost always, there is some link between the organising team and the priest who serves the area, even if he cannot attend every preparatory meeting.

2. *Starting-points*

If, for ease of comparison, we examine why the first assembly in a diocese came to be organised, we find that the reasons given by the 62 dioceses which answered the question fall into the following 2 groups:

(a) *Pressure of circumstances*. This covers cases where the priest is ill, has died, has left, or is away; is overburdened because he has new areas to serve, or has to be temporarily absent because of a diversified ministry; cases where preparations are being made to replace a priest of advanced years; where travel is difficult or villages are hard to reach. 17 of the 62 dioceses did not specifically mention the lack of a priest.

(*b*) *A pastoral project.* This group of reasons complements the previous set and covers the availability of trained group leaders or of lay people who are both free and willing to take charge of an assembly; the desire to stimulate the laity into taking up their responsibilities, to prepare them for doing so, and to put co-responsibility into practice (with frequent references in the diocesan reports to the 1973 Assembly of Bishops text *'Tous responsables dans l'Eglise?'* mentioned above); the wish to preserve a living local community; to avoid depriving old people and children, and to adapt the gathering to the local people; and a desire on the part of priests not to be 'swallowed up' by religious services.

To the 1977 survey we can now, in 1979, add over a hundred working papers, from many different parts of France, which have been compiled in preparation for a national colloquium by people who organise or are in charge of Sunday assemblies. A noteworthy fact, in so far as half of them at least were written by members of the laity, is that these papers give the same reasons for the establishment of assemblies as the 1977 survey.[3] We learn too that, in most cases, the first steps towards setting up the assembly were taken jointly by priest and laity. In others, the initiative came from the area priest, the vicars general or the episcopal vicars, or from the bishop. Less frequently, it sprang from the laity alone.

The papers' discussion of other aspects of the subject highlights a number of attitudes. They show a strong concern for young people from non-practising families. They express the fear that there will be no-one to take over from the organisers if they should leave the area or if there are no young people at the services. Lastly, there are those who are unwilling to go elsewhere to a service; their arguments reveal an inability to overcome deep-rooted local animosities, or reluctance to go the Church in a larger neighbouring township.

2. ROLES AND RESPONSIBILITIES

If the diocesan reports for the years 1971-77 and the complementary 1979 working papers are analysed, it becomes possible to show how the way in which members of a group relate to and interact with each other can improve. Similarly, the difficulties that are encountered can be identified.

1. *Participation in the service*

The change from a passive assembly of 'spectators' to a participatory assembly of responsible 'actors' is stressed repeatedly. It is reflected in the way people take part in the service; as one of the very varied descriptions puts it, '(They) sit closer to each other, are more ready to sing, and when necessary, speak to each other with less ceremony'. In the view of some informants, the change to an active assembly will make it possible for 'a new type of priest' to emerge.

Everything is, however, not perfect; membership of the assemblies is still too limited in range; so few young people come; as a result, some assemblies are no more than skeletons. There are not always enough group organisers. And some people long for the old days when they could leave it all to someone 'who organised everything because it was his job to do so'.

2. *The functions and responsibilities of the laity*

The papers collected in June 1979 show that lay people have taken on responsibility for the following activities, apart from the liturgical assemblies: religious education of the children (65 out of 114 replies), looking after parish premises (55), managing the parish finances (31), the collection (26), visiting the sick and the old (20), notices, newspapers, press committee (18), reception (12), preparation for the sacraments: baptism (3), marriage (2), communion (2), burials (3), assisting the priest with burials (3), prayer vigils when a death occurs (3), youth movements, other organisations (3), parish delegates (3). Once a member of the assembly has assumed responsibility for some aspect of the Sunday service, he will often go on to make a wider commitment to serving the parish community. But preparation for the sacraments still appears to be largely reserved for the priest.

Concentrating now on individual functions within the service, we find the papers using such terms as organiser or leader, reader, being in charge of singing or of the choir, coordinating the service, speaking the welcome, introducing the readings and—inevitably—'fetching the ciborium and giving communion'.

With some functions, however, there can be difficulties, since individuals are unwilling to take them on, and the assembly is reluctant to see them filled by a layman. Some assemblies will not have a layman give the homily or distribute communion. As for preparation for the sacraments, 'people do not like dealing with the laity; they feel as if they are facing a judge'. There is, too, the danger of becoming a 'pseudo-priest', of getting trapped in a role, and developing neo-clerical attitudes. These points show that it is not easy to break free of the old ways of thinking. But the role that causes the most noticeable difficulties is that of president of the assembly. Some would like it to be clearly seen for what it is, though they wish it to be filled discreetly, and not always by the same person. Others reject any idea of a president, since they do everything as a team; once again, the danger of appearing to be a 'pseudo-priest' is mentioned. Many of the reports stress the need for a principal organiser or coordinator. They seem to be mainly concerned that the service should run smoothly, and do not deal specifically with the strictly theological issue.

3. *The ordained presbyteral ministry: images and expectations*

'Both the meaning and the function' of the ordained minister are 'appearing in a new light'. The days when he was 'the man who saw to everything', 'the pillar of the parish', are over. Now, his duties are more diverse: serving the parish community, youth work, Catholic action meetings, working sessions. In consequence, his image is more varied. He is seen as the dynamic group leader; as educator, group adviser, linkman—with the diocese, almost obligatorily; as a rallying-point and a sign of unity.

He is expected to give liturgical, biblical and theological training, to be the guarantee that the liturgical service is authentic and that what is said and done there is orthodox. (The terms used in the documents are revealing; they speak of reassurance, of endorsement, of being 'covered'; of a sense of security when he is there . . .)

He should live among the people, 'so that the message of the gospel can be spread in conversation about concrete, everyday matters'. His role is seen too as one of encouragement, of spiritual support, as an opening onto the gospel. But elsewhere in the papers, we read that he should not arbitrarily impose his own views or, 'on the pretext that he wants to do something else with the time', too readily oppose a plan worked out by a team.

3. QUESTIONS AND FUTURE PROSPECTS

There can be no doubt that when lay Christians take charge of a Sunday assembly, they reach a deeper understanding of it. But not all are yet convinced of the value of the services; they wonder too whether consecrated bread can fittingly and meaningfully be shared other than during mass. Many of the papers stress that this practice can be meaningful in a Sunday assembly only if there is mass at the same place, and on a Sunday, in alternate weeks, or at least once a month. There is still a strong desire for the Eucharist. Furthermore, even if the Sunday services appear to be more satisfying than the mass—and often follow much the same pattern—the facts seem to show that they are not being confused with it, as is feared by priests in particular. (Given their frequent similarity to the mass, and the fact that the celebrations are not simply meetings for prayer, but Christian services of Sunday worship, it is understandable if people wonder which are their key moments.)

The development of assemblies has opened up a number of questions. The 3 we shall focus on concern both the organisation of the groups and unity within the Church; they are therefore vital for the future of assembly communities.

(*a*) In some very small parishes, the numbers and composition of the population are such that it can no longer form a separate unit. The inhabitants of these areas will probably have to overcome their desire to be independent, and join with several other villages to organise the services needed for the life of the whole group. This would not necessarily make them dependent on a larger settlement or township, but would allow them to take part in their local assembly and in more broadly based gatherings alternately.

(*b*) Closer involvement of the laity in the details of preparing and running the Sunday service usually leads to the community becoming self-organising. As a result of these changes, there is a marked alteration in the manner and content of communication within the assembly; in particular, differences of age, milieu, class and political opinion come to the fore. Another result of the changes is that new areas have been opened up for free discussion—an unwonted freedom for a flock trained to other ways. So unity may be threatened and leadership become—sometimes radically—controversial.

(*c*) A large number of Christians involved in assemblies are hoping that this alternative form of Sunday practice can be recognised as contributing to the building up of the Church. Indeed, they are going further and are asking whether, within these communities, there could not be ministries through which, with local support and cooperation, the Word could be proclaimed and communion within the Church be accomplished.

The fairly rapid spread of Sunday assemblies in France should not be given exaggerated importance. But we know that in the next 30 years, many parts of the country will be short of priests. If both these elements in the situation are given due weight, one cannot avoid the conclusion that priestless assemblies are the point around which the related and quite fundamental questions of the presbyteral ministry and the presidency of the Eucharist are going to arise. They will arise, furthermore, not at the periphery, but at the very centre of the institutional Church, and in the most concrete manner possible.

From another angle, these questions will involve identifying 'potential Eucharistic communities', in theory and on the ground. On the one hand, such communities should not automatically be equated with the remnants of our old parishes. But on the other, they should probably not just be equated with affinity groups in which the privileges of the least culture-bound sections of the community would have free play.

A further question still concerns the optimum size of the communities, relations between their members, and the way they should be grounded in the social environment. All this is yet to be thought out and put into practice. One of the more important aspects of the assembly groups appears to be their openness towards people who differ in the manner and degree of their commitment to the Church. Some groups are already working in this area.

In conclusion, may one hope that those who preside over the Church will ask themselves whether there would not be grave consequences if, in the near future, they were to risk depriving these communities of a most necessary ministry[4]; a ministry that would allow them, in communion with the bishops, and through baptism and the Eucharist particularly, to be a sign of the action of the Spirit and communion between the churches? May one hope too that, accepting the need for such a ministry, they will go further, and consider if it could not be entrusted to those who are proving themselves already in the service of existing communities?

Translated by Ruth Murphy

Notes

1. See our article 'Assemblées dominicales en l'absence de prêtre, situation en France et enjeux pastoraux' *La Maison-Dieu* 130 (1977) 78-79, where a detailed account of this survey will be found.

It is worth recalling that the assemblies are not without precedent in France, since there were meetings for prayer, without a priest, in the 1930s and during the Second World War. Similarly, both during the revolution and at the time of the Napoleonic Concordat there were 'substitute masses' which consisted in meetings for prayer and sometimes even celebration of the fore-mass, presided over individually or collectively by laymen with recognised spiritual gifts (see B. Plongeron, ed. *La Religion populaire, approches historiques* (Paris 1976) p, 144).

2. Assemblée plénière de l'épiscopat français '*Tous responsables dans l'Eglise?*' (Paris 1973).

3. The unusual nature of this collection of statements and observations deserves special notice. The contributors are people who, lay or priest, are all actively involved, in positions of responsibility, with this work of building up the

Church. Their commitment is practical, *ad hoc*; yet for the time being at least, force of circumstance has put them in a position both to speak out and, within limits, to act on their own initiative. Hence the somewhat mixed nature of their comments.

4. 'It is impossible to unite men within a single religious denomination whether true or false unless they are kept together by means of some system of symbols or sacraments in which they all share': thus St Augustine, quoted by St Thomas Aquinas when he is arguing the need for the sacraments seen in their social dimension rather than in their effects on the individual. T. Gilby, OP ed. *Summa Theologiae* (London and New York 1964-76) LVI, 3a, 61, 1.

Karl Derksen

A Voice from Holland

THE Christian Churches in Holland are entering the eighties with a great variety of parishes and communities. One should realise especially that side by side with the officially, canonically established parishes, there is a growing number of informal communities. Many of the latter belong to a nationwide movement of grass-roots communities and radical parishes.[1] Against the background of such variety in the formation of Christian communities, it is no easy matter to report on the practice of the ministry. For the sake of clarity I shall describe two developments which are closely related, but nevertheless divergent. In the first section I shall describe the renewal movement within the official Catholic community in Holland; in the second, the movement of grass-roots communities and radical parishes.

1. THE RENEWAL MOVEMENT

Since the middle of the sixties there has been in evidence a profound process of reflection on the ministry, especially within the Roman Catholic community of Holland. This re-thinking was stimulated by an inquiry conducted in 1968, which brought to light factual information on many aspects of the service of the ministry. The method in this inquiry was from the start different from the one used by Vatican II in its Decree on the Service and Life of the Priests *Presbyterorum Ordinis,* which had started much more from abstract theological principles.[2] During the year 1969 many lay people and priests discussed the report entitled 'Towards a fruitful and renewed functioning of the ministry', which in January of the same year had been on the agenda of the Pastoral Council of the Catholic Church in Holland. Any one who re-reads the papers and the minutes of the discussions now is struck by the high hopes and deep faith with which many women and men were then looking for new forms of the ministry. In broad outline, the desire was felt to examine critically both the contents of the ministry and the life of the minister, as both had been historically conditioned. Time and time again the minutes mention the desirability of married priests and of the admission of women to the ministry. At the same time great emphasis is laid on not wanting to break the bond with the universal Church. The bishops, who abstained when the various recommendations touching on the separation of priesthood and celibacy were brought to the vote, promised to present to Rome the wishes of a large section of the Catholics of Holland. Subsequently Cardinal Alfrink had various talks with the pope and with a number of cardinals (among whom was Willebrands). With the express wish that conversations between the Dutch episcopate and Rome be continued, the question was referred to the Synod of Bishops of 1971.[3] Meanwhile the point of view of Dutch catholics was being both supported and rejected in other countries. It was not, for that matter, a question of mainly pragmatic importance; everywhere people expressed a wish for an intensive biblical and theological study. The non-catholic observers at the Dutch Pastoral Council had also underlined this wish.

From the beginning of the seventies the pressure exerted by the central authorities of the Church on the developments of the Catholic community in Holland became heavier and heavier. This made unbiased and open-minded practice and discussion of the ministry more difficult. Nonetheless, in all kinds of parishes, people continued searching and experimenting, refusing in most cases to depart from the narrow road of canon law. In almost every instance an unmarried ordained male person presided at the Eucharistic celebrations. In cases where it was difficult to find such a person, people preferred to resort to another type of celebration. In cases where the Eucharist was indeed led by a married priest or non-priest, male or female, this was more often than not in a group belonging to the movement of grass-roots communities and radical parishes. I shall return to this later in this article.

In 1975 a report was published about the ecclesiastical ministry by an ecumenical commission, which had previously, in 1972, published one about the Eucharist and the (Protestant) Lord's Supper. The reactions of the different policy-making bodies of the churches to this report was frankly disappointing. They did not pay any attention to the encounter of faith which had slowly grown within the commission; it is precisely this kind of disappointment that regularly assails believing men and women. People come to the conclusion that certain practical steps are necessary, e.g., having a woman or a married priest preside at the Eucharist, or the celebration of an ecumenical Eucharist (Lord's Supper); and when they take such practical steps they have to face tensions and conflicts with the authorities of their respective churches. In Holland we are fortunate enough to know that at least a few bishops in their heart of hearts would like to support these experiments. At times some progress is made, as happened recently in a certain area of the city of Utrecht, where the assembled pastoral workers chose a woman as the leader of their team. After initial hesitation, the bishop accepted this. In Holland, too, a relatively high number of women and men are actively engaged in tasks which the Christian community feels called upon to fulfil as a consequence of its understanding of the gospel. Now and again one can hear the voice of these committed people, who in spite of all kinds of frustrations have not given up their struggle. Such was the case at the National Pastoral Council during its session of October 1978. (This Council allows regular deliberations to take place between representatives of the Dutch Catholic Community and their bishops, and was constituted when Rome would not allow a more authoritative body to be formed.) On that occasion they worded their intentions as follows: 'We wish to make very clear that our aim is to make the ecclesiastical ministry accessible to: married men; to women; and to priests who marry or who are married'.[5] This time too their statement gave rise to an emotionally charged discussion, and once more it became clear how problems arising from regulations of canon law tend to obscure a deeper view of the mission entrusted to the community of Jesus.

2. THE MOVEMENT OF GRASS-ROOTS COMMUNITIES AND RADICAL PARISHES

This movement in Holland does not want to have its convictions and practices as believers frustrated by interventions from higher authority, including those concerned with the exercise of the ministry. It wishes to continue in a free and liberating way the renewal movement which originated round Vatican II. This movement embraces groups at grass-roots level that were formed partly in the late sixties, while others are still being formed every day. They hardly ever were the direct outcome of a conflict with the official Churches. Often they simply want to take a different, a quicker and more direct road than the one followed by the churches. Only in one or two cases a group owes its origin to the fact that the official Church cut its links with them. In May 1979, at the Annual Assembly of this movement, a text was adopted which contains the following declaration about Christian communities: 'We opt consciously and purposely for the formation of groups and communities at the ground level, in the conviction that the vision of justice cannot be borne aloft by isolated individuals. The community must be formed around celebration, reflection and action. In such a community there ought to be room for all the dimensions of human existence: for pain, loneliness, joy, expectation,

D

sorrow and despair. For only a person who has been comforted can mean something to his fellowman. In our celebrations the vision of 'this world to be renewed' is kept before our eyes, with songs, testimonies, readings from the scriptures, poems, political information and the breaking of the bread. In these communities one finds biblical reflection, political deliberation and mutual pastoral care. They engage in action and take a stand'.[6] The description just given originated from the concrete practice of the communities participating in the movement. The ministries arise naturally from the various tasks which the communities undertake as their own. A community has not only a right to such ministries; they are absolutely necessary if the community is to remain faithful to its messianic task.

An example to illustrate this. In the autumn of 1977 about 30 men and women belonging to different Churches met in the city of Utrecht. A number of them had already left their churches or had become impatient with the slow developments within their respective parishes or Protestant communities. They wished to give a new and more explicit impetus to the renewal movement of the sixties. They felt a need for a deepening of the faith, for formation and celebrations, in which the problems of every individual and of society at large could be seen in their mutual relationship. In the spring of 1978 the moment arrived for those needs to be met. A number of men and women accepted responsibility for a number of tasks. Some began to prepare celebration, others a programme of formation, and yet others to invite people from the Third World to come and speak to them. The different tasks which this new community had set itself gave rise to a number of services and ministries. Every member who is willing to participate in the building up of the community is in priciple called to those tasks. Ecclesiastical origin, sex or state of life play no part. This does not mean that the members neglect to reflect regularly on what in Christian tradition has been done or taught. Very early on it was found meaningful for example to say a eucharistic prayer at the meetings and to give one another bread and wine. The group also continues with their discussions on the ministry. Meanwhile, however, the community has to be ready for service both towards its own members and to the world outside, and for this, responsible leaders or ministers are needed.

By no means all grass-roots communities combine their meetings with the celebration of the Eucharist or the Lord's Supper. The 'De Vier Handen' group in Groningen, for example, has suspended the celebration of the Eucharist/Lord's Supper. A strong awareness of Holland's complicity in the hunger suffered in many parts of the world causes the members to refrain from taking bread and wine, signs of willingness to share with others. According to them the right of the community to celebrate the Eucharist/Lord's Supper can under certain circumstances no longer be exercised except by renouncing or postponing it.

Whatever the form the meetings take, either freely using bread and wine, or diffidently renouncing these signs so heavy with meaning, the conviction is growing within the movement of grass-roots communities and radical parishes in Holland that it is in the first place the community itself that is the bearer of all ministries and tasks. In the community of St Dominic in Amsterdam more than a thousand people belonging to different Churches have been meeting every Sunday for the last ten years. When a public discussion was held there recently about the ministry, very many people gave their opinion that it is the community as a whole that has the first responsibility for the preaching of the word and the administration of the sacraments. Against this background the question of the right of the community to have a priest is formulated and answered in a manner quite different from that when the existing Church order is left unquestioned. 'We have shown that it can be done differently, not that it should be done differently: that will become clear as time goes on. We have shown that the community will itself decide how it wishes to celebrate the Lord's Supper/Eucharist. While the leaders of the different Christian Churches are still arguing about the possibility of celebrating the Lord's Supper together, we have shown that we are already doing it, like so many others. We have shown that it is not the ministry which is of paramount importance, but the community.' Thus writes a spokesman of a basic community at Heemstede to a reformed clergyman who had raised objections to the practices of that community.

Within the movement experiments with new forms of service of the ministry are in full development. There is a good deal of writing and thinking being done about it and the various groups exchange their experiences with one another. As an example of this we could mention a study session entitled: '*Basis en Ambt*' (Grass-roots Communities and the Ministry) at Beverwijk on 9 December 1978, organised by the radical parish Ijmond on the occasion of the sacerdotal jubilee of the 'pastor' of that community, who, because of his marriage, would, according to canon law, no longer be allowed to preside at the Eucharist. It proved to be a fruitful day: the 400 participants heard from about 10 grass-roots communities how they were dealing with the question of the ministry. One group from Rotterdam, known for its strong criticism of the established order, declared: 'The Christian community is, together with its ministers, the priestly people of God (1 Peter 2). In the Jewish-Christian tradition this priestly people has always had, at least as an undercurrent, a prophetic, that is a communicating function. It is true that the dialogue between God and mankind has been in God's direction hierarchically structured from within the Church. But the dialogue from within the Church towards the masses is being ignored more and more. We know how God's word sounds, but we can no longer express it in the language of the masses. . . . We shall have to learn how to speak their language. . . . Neither the hierarchy nor the Eucharist are in the first instance decisive for the bond of love that keeps Christians together. What is decisive is their self-sacrificing and radical commitment to the rights of those who have become ever more rightless and helpless.'[7] An ecumenical religious community, which is itself the heart of a new kind of community, came forward with an extensive reflection on the ministry, based on its own experience. I quote: 'As long as unity has not been achieved, we live from an ecclesiastical point of view in a permanent state of emergency. Following practices that have already established themselves, we do not shrink from handing "ministerial" tasks to our people . . .; in the "partial ministry" the general priesthood of all the faithful is actualised and condensed. The ministry is much more a messianic mandate and task than an ecclesiastical function which involves certain mandates. . . . We must not obstruct Christ's salvific presence among men by restrictive Church rules; neither must we dismember that presence needlessly by each going our own way, without taking into account other traditions and experiences. . . . The ministry must not be allowed to become a puzzle that constantly causes us headaches; it must be what it is: the hand of Christ being extended to all men.'[8]

Edward Schillebeeckx had been invited by the movement of grass-roots communities and radical parishes in order to listen to these reports and then reflect on them in the light of tradition and theology. He sketched a very varied picture in the light of the New Testament and argued that as far as this section of the Bible is concerned, there exists a right of the community to have ministers and to celebrate the eucharist; and that this takes precedence over the norms of admission to the ministry which the Church for that matter can and may lay down.

In Holland it has been clear for a long time that there is a crisis in the ministry. Many say this openly and it is admitted by Church leaders. Studies on this problem are published regularly.[9] Meanwhile there is sufficient information available from the rest of the world to be able to say that the crisis is general. Everywhere experiments are going on with new forms of ministry. In the grass-roots communities of Holland this is being done freely, in a way that leads to liberation.

Translated by B. J. Welling

Notes

1. The title used for the movement in this translation is the one used so far in English texts. As a result of a recent re-formulation of principles, the movement has slightly altered its Dutch name to 'Basisbeweging van kritische groepen en gemeenten in Nederland'. The Movement has its secretariat at: Tolsteegsingel 33, 3582 AH-Utrecht, Holland, and publishes a newsletter (called *Informatiebrief*).

2. See also: *Balans van de Nederlandse Kerk* (Bilthoven 1975), especially R. van Kessel 'Theologie en ambtsbediening sinds het Tweede Vatikaans Concilie' pp. 137-173.

3. See also: W. Goddijn *De Beheerste Kerk, Uitgestelde revolutie in R. K. Nederland* (Amsterdam/Brussels 1973) pp. 191-197.

4. *Archief van de Kerken*, Nr. 14 (8 June 1975) col. 588 etc.

5. *Informatiebulletin*, Biltstraat 121, Utrecht, Jrg. 6, nr. 19, pp. 470-471.

6. From: *Eerste visie en program van de Basisbeweging van kritische groepen en gemeenten in Nederland,* p. 6.

7. *Basis en Ambt. Ambt in dienst van nieuwe gemeentevorming* (Bloemendaal 1979) p. 28. In this book are found the descriptions of the various experiences, the discussion on them and the theological reflection by Edward Schillebeeckx on 9 December 1978 at Beverwijk.

8. *Ibid.,* p. 16.

9. J. Roos *Vrijwilligers Kerk . . . Kerk van de toekomst* (Baarn 1978); W. Boelens *Tafal en Gastheer. Toenadering bij interkommunie em ambt* (Baarn 1979).

Joseph A. Komonchak

'Non-ordained' and 'Ordained' Ministers in the Local Church

THE recent development and flourishing of new forms and styles of 'non-ordained' ministry in the Church are rooted in several basic principles of the ecclesiology of Vatican II. The first is the Council's insistence on the unity of the Church and the responsibility of all its members for its mission. A second is the Council's effort to rehabilitate 'charismatic' ministries; it encouraged the Church to *expect* that the Holy Spirit would provoke a whole series of services and ministries which are not mediated by the hierarchy, whose role is much more discernment and coordination than delegation and subordination. Third, the Council focused attention on the local church, particularly the Eucharistic assembly, as the primary instance of the Church's self-realisation.

On the basis of such principles and in response to varying needs, churches throughout the world have since the Council evoked new forms and styles of ministry. Some of these continue efforts begun before the Council, while others have emerged or taken on new form and importance since. The initiative for most of them has been taken on local, diocesan or national levels. With the exception of the permanent diaconate and the official 'ministries' of lector and acolyte, Roman documents have confirmed more than they have initiated; and in fact *Ministeria quaedam* created more practical problems than it solved.[1]

There is no room here to describe the developments in their very varied detail. Suffice it to say that they range broadly over the whole of the Church's pastoral care: preaching and teaching, worship, service in the world, community-leadership. For most of the new ministries, 'ordination' has not been considered necessary; other forms of ecclesial authorisation, formal or not, liturgical or not, episcopal or not, have been

44

employed. The thousands of men and women thus introduced into the ministry are, therefore, considered to be 'non-ordained', and their 'lay' ministries are often said to be grounded in baptism and confirmation.

Many things can be said in favour of these developments. In the first place, they show that local churches are assuming responsibility for themselves. The 'clergy' no longer has a monopoly on the ministry; all the members of the community can assume a role in and for the Church. As a result, the churches now have many more ministries and ministers than before and have become much more effective and flexible ministerial bodies. Second, in most of these cases the local Church is the immediate and primary reference-point of ministry; and this restores a very important ecclesial truth. Third, and related to this, the developments reflect a more proper relationship between 'charism' (or 'vocation') and community than the one that prevailed in the past. Local communities, knowing their needs and discerning appropriate abilities in their members, call people to assume the needed ministries.[2] Finally, in general at least, the new ministers are giving a non-clerical demonstration of ministry, both in the technical sense that they are not members of the 'clergy' (now comprising only deacons, priests and bishops) and in the more important sense that their ministry is not bound to the celibate and class conditions which have traditionally marked the ministry.

But this positive assessment of recent developments in ministry must be tempered by the fact that many of them have been accompanied (or indeed prompted) by the shortage of priests. It is true that many of the new ministries have a far more secure ecclesiological foundation than that of supplying for the lack of priests and that they represent valuable developments which might otherwise not have taken place.[3] But it remains that the developments themselves and any attempt to evaluate them theologically are affected by the practical necessities caused by the decline in the number of priests now working or anticipated for the future.

For example, in many areas (Asia, Africa, Latin America, but also in Europe and the United States), 'laypeople' have had to be authorised to assume responsibilities for which presbyteral ordination was once considered to be necessary. They may now preach and teach, baptise, prepare for and witness marriages, provide (non-sacramental) ministries of reconciliation, assist the sick and dying, conduct funeral services, administer the Eucharist, lead Sunday-worship, and assume the regular leadership of the community: all of the roles normally entrusted to the ordained 'pastor'.

The theological questions raised by such cases are not avoided by noting that they are canonically exceptional or extraordinary. For, by all realistic expectations, they are likely to become the statistically 'normal' situation. If they become that, it is difficult to overestimate the potential significance of the change in the self-perception of the Church and of its ministries which will result. In these cases, the Church will be realising itself locally under the presidency of 'laypeople'. The ordinary Christian life of the people will not be expressed in and nourished by the sacraments of the Eucharist, reconciliation and anointing. A priest will come when he can, from without, to hear confessions, say mass, anoint the sick. In the process, willy-nilly, a different Church will be under construction, by means of a different ministry; and the changes inevitably introduced should not pass without comment or criticism.

In the cases under consideration—in which the 'non-ordained' regularly perform the functions of a 'pastor'—the controlling principle has been *salus animarum suprema lex*: in face of concrete need, unable to do otherwise, local churches have evoked these 'lay' ministries. Perhaps only those inclined to fear that an ecclesiastical revolution is thereby postponed will regret the application of that supreme rule. But on many other theological principles this development deserves serious criticism.

The first criticism is that in these situations the intrinsic and constitutive relationship between the Eucharist and the Church is endangered. That 'the Church makes the Eucharist, and the Eucharist the Church' was something like a first principle of Vatican II's ecclesiology. The *ekklesia* is precisely that, an assembly, and never more the assembly of God than when gathered to hear his Word and to be brought into communion with the death and resurrection of Christ. But in many of these cases it is impossible for the local church to gather as a Eucharistic assembly. Whatever may happen at their Sunday services without priests—and it would be incorrect to say that they have no religious and ecclesial significance—they are not the Eucharist. The assembly may pray and sing together; they may hear the Word of God proclaimed and preached; they may offer prayers of thanksgiving and petition; they may share communion: but they do not celebrate the Eucharist *actio* and the Church-constitutive *memoria Christi* is not reactualised for their appropriation. If the Council's Eucharistic ecclesiology was valid, then something central to the church is lost when a community lacks a priest. Moreover, that is also true even when a priest may stop by to celebrate mass; for then the celebrant is not a member of the local community, and his ability to lead them in their worship is greatly diminished. There need be no doubts about the 'validity' of such a Eucharist nor about its importance; but it should not be neglected that this is an imperfect Eucharist and an imperfect Christian assembly.

Second, in the situations we are considering, the integrity of the local church is also compromised, and it is hindered from developing a sense of itself as something more than an administrative unit of a larger whole.

The community may have the ability, on practical criteria of need, ability and discernment, to evoke and sustain all kinds of services and ministries; but this stops short of the one ministry which is symbolically (in the strong sense of this word) the most important, the leadership of its worship. *This* minister must be chosen by criteria and under conditions over which the local church has no control. It is here that the tensions within the ecclesiology of Vatican II now have their most visible practical effect.[4]

Third, the unity and integrity of the ministry are in a number of respects compromised. For one thing, these situations perpetuate the division of the ministry into two levels, that of the 'laity' and that of the 'clergy', of the 'unordained' and of the 'ordained'. The 'difference is essence' is realised as a 'difference in degree', and the possibility of an organic coordination of all ministries is postponed in favour of a hierarchical subordination, giving new strength to the regrettable disjunctions between 'charism' and 'office' and between ministry and community.

Futhermore, the newly developed situations reintroduce the disjunction between the 'power of orders' and the 'power of jurisdiction' which the Council sought to overcome.[5] In contrast to the Council's teaching that all 3 of the pastoral functions derive from the single source of ordination, here the regular pastoral responsibilities of preaching or teaching and leadership are established on other grounds and entrusted to people other than those who have the responsibility to lead the community's worship. The intrinsic links between Word, sacrament and community-leadership are thereby broken. (It is well to keep in mind that this inner connection between the functions of pastoral ministry is not simply a theological conclusion. It has its resonance and even its verification in the socio-psychological realities of ministry. There is an inner drive towards sacrament in the performance of ministry, well illustrated in the question asked by the African community-leader: 'When I have reconciled two Christians, why must I then have to appeal to a third party to absolve them?')[6]

Lastly, the significance of ordination itself is called into question. In the situations described, ordination has in effect been reduced to a matter of sacramental empowerment. This has already led many people, including bishops, to ask why men should be ordained deacons when these cannot do anything which 'laypeople' cannot do—a curiously 'functional' view of ordination, by the way, with the sacramental function the only one that counts. But this also happens with regard to the presbyterate. Some candidates for ministry will not present themselves for ordination simply because the presbyterate has been so reduced in scope and function. Others see ordination as a simple instrument of clericalisation or as another instance of male domination.[7] Underlying these and other complaints are the loss of the full meaning of ordination and the separation of the presbyteral ministry from the concrete life of a local congregation.

The effect of all this is to introduce a good deal of confusion on both the practical and the theoretical levels. A good deal of spontaneity and creativity is possible in all ministries except that of the presbyter. All of the other ministries can have their natural home in a local community; but the presbyterate must follow lines not laid down by the community but externally imposed. This, of course, skews the development and articulation of all the ministries. Ministries, after all, only make good practical sense when they are organically interrelated. Developments in one ministry, then, will affect all others, as will immobility in any one of them. A coherent pastoral ministry is not possible where one ministry—especially the central one—proceeds on one kind of principle and all others on another. In the present situation, neither the presbyterate nor the other ministries can be properly and effectively articulated. This particularly affects the presbyterate, a restructuring and rethinking of which, although required simply by the emergence of new 'lay' ministries, are prevented by the decline in numbers and the refusal to reconsider the conditions for its reception.

The theoretical issue can perhaps be introduced by remarking that the point here is not that priests should be doing all the functions which 'laypeople' are doing in these situations, but that those who are doing them ought to be priests. This is more than verbal cleverness. The Church's primitive practice, the classic ordination prayers, even Vatican II, all support the view that the leader of the community should be the leader of the Eucharist, rather than the other way around.[8] The issue is whether insertion into a concrete community should prevail over a theological definition of the presbyterate in terms of 'powers'. The earlier and better grounded view of presbyteral ordination has also the great advantage of coinciding with the community-priciples which now operate in the development and functioning of the 'non-ordained' ministries.

Practical solutions to the present difficulties, of course, will depend on many considerations. But theologians may contribute by working towards a greater consensus on the theology of ministry than is now available. Two suggestions may here be made about work that needs to be done.

First, more attention should be given to the similarities rather than to the differences between 'non-ordained' and 'ordained' ministries. Many theologians still work with a very sharp distinction between 'clergy' and 'laity' even when they are vindicating the rights of the 'laity'. But while everyone in the Church is called to service and even (in a broad sense of the term) to 'ministry', it remains that all regular ministries imply a certain differentiation among the members of the Church. This differentiation cannot be adequately established on the basis of baptism and confirmation, which are common to all members of the Church. Some differentiation within the Body of Christ attends all regular ministries, whether these be grounded in 'charism', 'vocation', 'ordination, 'consecration' or 'office'. From a sociological perspective (which should not be irrelevant to an ecclesiology), there is a good deal more in common among those terms than theologians often note. All the ministries belong to a single genus and operate on a continuum, insights which are simply obscured when, for whatever reasons, reflection on ministry begins with the distinction between 'clergy' and 'laity'.[9]

Similarly, theologians need to devote more attention to the similarities between ordination and other forms of ecclesial authorisation and reception. This should be possible without reviving the old idea of 'minor orders'. Theologians might begin by paying some attention to the concrete social, institutional, and psychological implications of all forms of ecclesial authorisation now in use, from local designation to episcopal ordination (or, for that matter, papal election). They might find that the best-grounded traditional theology of ordination is confirmed by the concrete social (ecclesial) significance attached to the various ways in which the Church provides itself with its many ministers. And this might lead to a bit more nuance when it comes to differentiating 'ordination' from the other processes of authorisation and reception. And a way might be found beyond some of the more sterile impasses that afflict the theology of ministry.[10]

In the meantime, people need to be ministered to. If we may be grateful that so many men and women are now presenting themselves for this work in the new ministries, we must also hope that the day is not too far off when their generosity and talent will be free to make the full and coherent contribution that is so badly needed.

Notes

1. See J. Komonchak 'The Permanent Diaconate and the Variety of Ministries in the Church' *Diaconal Quarterly* 3/3 (1977) 15-23, 3/4 (1977) 29-40, 4/1 (1978) 13-25.

2. See C. Wackenheim 'Les "nouveaux ministères": sortir de l'impasse' *Communautés et liturgies* 58 (1976) 3-14; H. Legrand 'L'avenir des ministères: bilan, defis, tâches' *Les Supplément* 124 (Feb. 1978) 21-48.

3. See L. de Vaucelles 'Le destin incertain des Assemblées dominicales sans prêtres' *Études* 349 (1978) 239-248.

4. See C. Duquoc 'Théologie de l'Eglise et crise du ministère' *Études* 350 (1979) 101-113.

5. See J. Neumann 'Wort und Sakrament nicht spalten!' *Orientierung* 40 (1976) 86-87; 'Die wesenhafte Einheit von Ordination und Amt: Priester und Laien im Dienst der Kirche' in *Der Priestermangel und seine Konsequenzen: Einheit und Vielfalt der kirchlichen Ämster und Dienste* ed. F. Klostermann (Düsseldorf 1977) pp. 95-128.

6. 'La question des ministères en Afrique' *Spiritus* 18 (1977) 344; see also P. D. Delanotte 'Catéchistes hier, responsables de communautés actuellement' *Spiritus* 18 (1977) 350-359.

7. See W. Kasper 'Die schädlichen Nebenwirkungen des Priestermangels' *Stimmen der Zeit* 195 (1977) 129-135.

8. See P.-M. Gy 'La théologie des prières anciennes pour l'ordination des évêques et des prêtres' *Revue des Sciences Philosophiques et Theologiques* 58 (1974) 599-617; H. J. Schulz 'Das liturgisch-sakramental übertragene Hirtenamt in seiner eucharistischen Selbstverwirklung nach dem Zeugnis der liturgischen Überlieferung' in *Amt und Eucharistie* (Paderborn 1973) pp. 208-255; H. Legrand 'La Présidence de l'Eucharistie selon la tradition ancienne' *Spiritus* 18 (1977) 409-431. The point is well argued also in C. Duquoc in the article cited in note 4.

9. See C. Wackenheim in the article cited in note 2, and also his article 'Esquisse d'une théologie des ministères' *Revue des Sciences Religieuses* 47 (1973) 3-26; H. Legrand 'Insertion des ministères de direction dans la communauté ecclésiale' *Rev. Droit Can.* 23 (1973) 225-254.

10. I am convinced that the theology of ministry will not be able to progress beyond its present impasses until theologians are willing to bring sociological sensitivities and tools to the study of the New Testament, the tradition and contemporary ecclesial practice.

Fritz Lobinger

The Right of the Community
to Develop in its Faith

THE statistical section of this issue shows that the majority of Christian communities in Africa lives most of the time without a priest. Meanwhile all over Africa community building has become the first priority in pastoral work and these communities have started to feel responsible themselves for their own needs. Lay leaders have emerged under many different names. They are called *bakambi* (leaders),[1] or *responsables de communautés*[2] or any of over a hundred other different names.[3] It is no surprise that in this situation, again and again the question has been asked why some of these leaders could not preside over the celebration of the Eucharist.

1. THE FEAR OF ORDINATION

The discussion has developed in a strange way. Nobody seems to doubt that proven lay leaders could in fact administer the sacraments, but there is very much hesitation about a proper sacramental ordination of such men. Some look instead for rather strange alternatives such as a 'pastoral delegation to preside over the eucharist' or being 'recognised by the bishop—and in no way tied to the ordained ministry', a 'Eucharist without a priest' led by people who are 'in communion' with the bishop,[4] or presiding over the Eucharist without becoming a member of the presbyterium,[5] or for an 'indult' to widen the function of lay leaders.[6]

There are reasons for this fear of ordination. There is the fear that ordained men could not be removed from office if found unsuitable. There is also the fear that ordination would constitute an irresistible temptation to status-seeking, or the fear that this would mean a clerical-

51

isation of lay people, or that the ordination of one person would decrease the present wide involvement of many members of the community.

Besides this there is in Africa a great number of people who oppose in principle any ordination of proven lay leaders while at the same time they wholeheartedly support the movement of community building and lay responsibility. Some of them think that there is still hope that the present shortage of priests will end. Others oppose it because they feel that it would cause an unknown avalanche of consequences. They feel that it is the task of the older churches to try out such a new step first.

It is true that there are many countries in Africa where the major seminaries are completely full. But it is also true that even this present strong flow of vocations will not be sufficient to make up for the over 70 per cent of the present priests who are expatriates and will not be replaced by other missionaries. These will have to be replaced by local vocations during the next 20 years while over the same period a big increase of Church membership is expected. There is also the impact of urbanisation which until now has not yet been felt in many areas of Africa, but which will become an increasing obstacle to vocations.

There are therefore good reasons for continued attempts to clarify the confused discussion about the possibility of ordaining lay leaders. In this discussion the key question seems to be the possible harmful effects of the ordination of such leaders and we will therefore first concentrate on this aspect. This will lead us to a deeper understanding of the right of the community to have priests.

2. WITHHOLDING ORDINATION IS THE WRONG SOLUTION

Ordination is considered irreversible and this makes many hesitate to ordain proven lay leaders. But is this not a parallel to the early Church, when the irreversibility of baptism led to a strict discipline and this in turn led very many to hesitate about being baptised and rather to live as Christians without being baptised? These life-long catechumens postponed baptism to the moments before death. The Church of today rejects this practice and thinks it is better to take the risk of failures after the irreversible sacramental rite. In a similar way we should avoid the idea of 'life-long catechumens for ordination'.

Irreversible ordination makes many fear that unsuitable people could then not be removed from office. But does not our present wide experience with lay leaders show that it is often difficult to remove even the unordained leaders? We must certainly find ways of removing unsuitable leaders, especially since local leaders cannot be transferred and will remain in the same congregation all their life. But we need better methods than avoiding ordination. Education for team-work is a much better method, education for the rotation of office-bearers, education for limited exercise of office even without any misconduct, education for communal responsibility and for much interaction between community and leaders, these measures have proved good and are a better safeguard against wrong leaders than the function-without-ordination approach.

It is also feared that ordination would clericalise people. This term can mean many things. It can stand for monopoly and this is certainly a danger to community building. But again, withholding ordination is a weak safeguard against it, since monopoly can occur even without ordination, and there are better antidotes against it, as outlined above. Clericalism can also mean being aloof from other people. What makes a person behave in this way is not ordination itself but being the only person who is in an exposed and central position. If leaders are trained to work and plan in teams and if a great variety of other ministries exist next to the ordained ones, then this danger is greatly reduced.

It is further feared that the ordination of a few will decrease wide involvement of the whole community. The whole community might become passive as soon as one person is ordained. But again, it would not be the effect of ordination as such, but of a wrong way of singling out one lone person, or a wrong way of training such people apart from the community. Experience has shown convincingly that this harmful process can be avoided. There are communities which have had a group of deacons for several years, and yet there still exists a wide variety of other ministries besides them. It all depends on the way in which ministries are introduced. We can also learn from the experience of other churches, which already have 'tent-maker priests' and where their ordination did not decrease the wide involvement of the whole congregation.

Those who fear all the above ill-effects of ordination and who therefore look for ways of avoiding the ordination of lay leaders, will of course look for theological justifications for this. They may point at some instances in the early Church, where confessors who escaped alive from martyrdom presided over the Eucharist without ordination. The early Church did this because those men had identified with Christ and with the Church to such an extent that a subsequent ordination would have appeared as a weaker manifestation than martyrdom. Our present case is exactly the opposite. We have Christian communities with leaders of whom we are not sure whether there is sufficient identification with Christ. In this case it is wrong to seek ways of dispensing from the ritual and from the irreversible manifestation of acting in Christ's name. There is not less need for ordination but more.

One can come to the same conclusion through practical experience. We went to some communities which have teams of self-supporting deacons and interviewed the members of the community and the deacons themselves. What did ordination mean to those men, since they did nothing new after ordination? All they did now they had already done before being ordained. 'The most difficult thing for me was to commit myself', said one deacon. He had been a voluntary helper in the community for many years, and had worked in such a reliable way that he was nominated for ordination. But ordination meant a commitment which went beyond all this. Therefore even if our theology and our Church law would permit us to avoid ordination, we should ask for retaining it. We should not look at it only as a prescribed prerequisite, but as a means of growth and witness. We should be more afraid of Eucharistic celebrations presided over by poorly committed Christians than of leading such Christians towards fuller commitment through formation for ordination.

We can look at the same question from another angle, again from practical experience, but this time from the priest's view. In which cases do priest conduct more training: where they ask people just to act as helpers, or where they try to build up a permanent group of leaders who are solemnly commissioned? There may be exceptions, but generally there will be more training where people are led to identify with their task in a definite way. This will be still more true where not only lay ministries are at stake but the ordained ministry. We should not try to run away from the challenging task of building up men for irreversible ordination. Not only a challenge appears before us, but also a new horizon and a new possibility of growth.

3. THE COMMUNITY TOO MUST DEVELOP

Not only the candidates for ministry will have to grow in faith, but their community has to grow with them if it is to accept them. A little incident can illustrate this. In one of the congregations which has newly ordained deacons, a baby was to be baptised by one of them. But the parents refused vehemently: 'What, our child is to be baptised by a shoemaker?' The community had gone through a long process of re-thinking and had accepted the deacons, but that one couple had not participated in this process. In our present Church structure the highly trained priest belongs to a different class of people. He lives in a way quite different from the others. Therefore his ministry is often interpreted in terms of class and prestige. Douglas Webster has shown that Protestant congregations who had the tent-maker pattern of ministry were eager to get a full-time minister because it gives prestige to a congregation if it has a 'real' minister.[8] These examples show how much a Christian community has to learn, or in what ways it has to grow spiritually if it is to accept an ordained minister who is one of themselves and remains such, instead of being cared for by a minister who is a 'professional' coming from outside. A different vision of the Church is at stake, not just the providing of the sacraments. If a community has learnt to prefer that some of its own members grow in faith to such an extent that the universal Church accepts them as links to the universal Church, if it has learnt to understand that their ordination means that the gospel has taken root in a deeper way in this community and has become more incarnated in it, then this community is surely closer to the New Testament notion of Church than one which looks down on leaders because they are 'just like us'. The age-old desire to have religious leaders who are set apart for religious duties gives the impression of being a holy desire, but it is not the type of holiness which we are taught in the New Testament. Not only the vision of 'Church' is involved here, but also the idea of the world, our vision of what a secular profession is. The desire to have religious leaders who do not at the same time practise a secular profession again looks like a holy desire, but it is not the Christian vision of the relation between God and world. A Christian community which accepts ordained leaders who remain in their daily work, and accepts them expressly because this signifies God's presence in this world, such a community has not just solved the provision of sacraments, but has made a special contribution to the preaching of the incarnation.

It has become clear that the development of an ordained ministry within each Christian community is much more than finding substitutes for a dwindling clergy. It is a growth process of the whole community in its faith. This puts the whole question of a 'right of a community to a priest' into a different light. Surely there is the right to receive the sacraments, and there is the right to lead a full sacramental life, but there is also the right and even the obligation to complete the process of incarnating the gospel in each local Church. This process includes the development of a fully responsible ordained ministry in each community.

4. PRINCIPLES FOR IMPLEMENTATION

For the practical implementation of the above vision the following principles have emerged from experience.

1. Community building must be the starting-point and the continual basis for the development of all ministries. Ministries should not be an aim in themselves. Also the pace of development should be determined by the changing consciousness of the community and not by a pre-determined syllabus or a fixed schedule of 'intervals'. African communities can build on a rich tradition of community life and will not take long to build on it the consciousness of a Christian community.

2. We should never ordain one lone lay leader, but only teams. The

E

principle may seem hard, but has proved itself in practice. Even if there is an excellent candidate in a community, he should not be ordained until there are more.

3. Training should take place mainly in the local parish and through the local priest. Centralised training should only be complementary to this local training. The reason is again that the candidates should not develop away from the community but with it and with their priest.

Many priests and bishops have expressed the fear that a development as outlined above would make the present priests redundant. The opposite is true, they would definitely be needed as the spiritual centre of all these communities and of their ordained and unordained leaders. They would be needed as coordinators, animators and trainers, but first of all as men who could lead others to a deep commitment to Christ.

Notes

1. Described in many publications, e.g., 'Community Leaders in Kinshasa—Zaire' in *Pro Mundi Vita, Ministries and Communities* (1976) 1-8.

2. See the dossier 'La Question des ministères en Afrique' in *Spiritus* 18 (1977) 339-364. English-speaking Africa does not have an equivalent term.

3. A. Shorter-E. Kataza *Missionaries to Yourselves, African Catechists Today* (London 1972) p. 73.

4. All quotations from J. M. Ela 'Ecclesial Ministry and the Problems of the Young Churches' *Concilium* 106 (1977) 50.

5. P. Lefebvre 'Présidence des communautés chrétiennes et présidence de l'eucharistie' *Spiritus* 18 (1977) 359-364.

6. The *AMECEA Plenary Session of 1970* decided against introducing the permanent diaconate and to ask for such an indult instead. Conference Record 'The Priest in Africa Today' p. 38.

7. T. D. Verryn published an assessment of the 47 self-supporting priests and deacons who existed in the Anglican Church of Malawi and South Africa in 1971, in *Missionalia* 4 (1976) 12-40 (31 Fourteenth Street, Menlo Park, Pretoria). A similar report is included in P. M. Miller *Equipping for Ministry in East Africa* (Herald Press 1969).

8. D. Webster *Patterns of Part-time Ministry in some Churches in South America* (World Dominion Press 1964) p. 16.

PART III

Theological Reflections

Severino Dianich

The Ordained Ministry in Rites and Actions

1. THE IMPORTANCE OF TERMINOLOGY

THE WORD 'priest' immediately conjures up the whole spectrum of the world of ritualism. The idea of priesthood suggests images of temples and altars, awakens memories of slow processions and solemn chants, calls up sensations of drowsiness induced by the smell of incense and the feeling of bowing down before the sacred. Here things have no meaning in themselves, but only in reference and allusion to other realities, hidden from man and kept secret in the mystery of the Godhead. Their efficacy is something peculiar to themselves, since the relationship between their cause and effect depends on the unquestionable will of the Supreme Being.

In rites, man and society affirm the basic meaning of life, and the institution of the priesthood guarantees mediation between the people taking part and the 'world of Power'. With the breaking-away of the Church from Hebraism and the decline of paganism, the place of the old priestly caste was taken over spontaneously by the presbyteral-episcopal ministry, which from the cultural standpoint came to be established on the impressive foundations left by the priestly tradition of the order preceding it. Hence, despite the fact that the New Testament clearly opposes Christian priesthood to the old ritualism, there is a sort of linguistic inflexibility that makes it difficult to speak of priesthood without reference to the ritual images of the priestly institution fixed in our culture.

It is of course true that the Church has its own ritual tradition. It is equally true that our relationship with God can only be one based on his election and his grace, and can only affect us through signs that witness to the *actio Dei*, signs that transcend the ordinary power of human actions to signify and bring about. But in Christian faith our encounter with God is rooted in the human experience of Christ irrespective of any ritual acts: 'Everyone knows (Our Lord) came from Judah, a tribe which Moses did not even mention when dealing with priests' (Heb. 7:14). In the Letter to the Hebrews the old liturgical apparatus of the Temple becomes a sort of overall metaphor for illustrating how the mystery of our communion with God is fulfilled in Christ. The priesthood has been 'appointed to act for men in their relations with God, to offer gifts and sacrifices for sins' (5:1). But we must not forget that 'bulls' blood and goats' blood are useless for taking away sins' (10:4). If we are still saved, it is because gifts and sacrifices are no longer the blood of victims, but Christ's obedience to the Father (10:5-14). So when we talk of Christ as priest, we mean that he carries out the work of the priesthood; he does this, however, not through the means proper to the priesthood, i.e., rites, but through the actions of his own life. In the same way it is his will that the Church should enact rites, but its priesthood does not consist primarily in a ritual apparatus, but rather in its being in Christ, living and working in imitation of him.

To sum up, our priestly terminology operates on three semantic levels each distinct from the others. If we follow the line of the historical memory of cultural continuity in pre-Christian and Christian ritual, priestly terminology can be used as a metaphorical language: the high priest propitiating his own entrance into the sanctuary by sacrificing the victim on the altar in the name of all the people is an 'image' of the mystery of salvation completed by Christ's dying in obedience to the will of the Father. If, however, we try to bypass reference to pre-Christian ritual and think exclusively in terms of the priesthood of Christ, then the words used need an existential, not a ritual, interpretation: they must describe the teachings and actions through which the unique human experience of Christ brings about our communion with God. In the same vein, the Church is a priestly people: 'by her relationship with Christ, the Church is a kind of sacrament or sign of intimate union with God' (LG 1a), by virtue of its faith and its following of Christ. Finally, 'priesthood' can be used to refer to Christian ritual, as an essentially new reality concerned with the priesthood of actions: rite has meaning only as a calling to mind of the mystery of what Christ was and did in his life on earth, which the Church celebrates only through its faith and unity with him.

2. RITE AND CHARISM IN THE ORDAINED MINISTRY

When the Church celebrates the rites of its 'seven sacraments', it seeks an efficacy in their mystery proportionate to the *actio Dei* rather than to their human capacity for imitating Christ. The ministry of the pastors of the Church has its origin in the rite of ordination and its culmination in that of the Eucharist. In this respect it must be seen as an essentially different priesthood from that of the rest of the faithful. This gives rise to the question: What vital reality do these ritual aspects relate to? The question is necessary because the ritualism of the ministry must relate either to the life of Christ or to that of the Church and the particular role it has to play in that. It is only through an understanding of the existential meaning of the charism of order that it is possible to appreciate its necessary derivation from ordination and how it reaches the apex of its meaning in the consecration of the Eucharist. If, as Vatican II states, the liturgy is the source and summit of the life of the Church, we need to examine the river that flows from ordination and the mountain whose peak is the Eucharistic consecration.

The existential sacramentality of the Church takes different forms and varies in degree: certain activities can be more or less redolent of communion with God; certain persons more or less Christ-like, certain actions more or less effective in the development of the new man, certain undertakings more or less apt to direct history toward the Kingdom. No-one, however, is in a position to judge the degree of sacramentality attaching to this or that manifestation of the life of the Church: their differences belong to the realm of secrets of conscience or spread over broad historical courses that can only be evaluated from a great distance. What we can judge, however, is whether a particular component of the life of the Church is only one aspect of the infinite riches and variety of its gifts, or whether it is a basic constitutive component of the Church itself. On this level the ordained ministry can be allotted its proper place: it does not represent the highest degree of the sacramentality of the Church, which would be a holiness possessed to a degree of fullness that enabled it to mediate the salvation of others, but it is a component the Church absolutely cannot do without. It might be possible for a mystic or a politician to command a degree of efficacy in making the Church the sacrament of communion with God far higher than that of a pope or a priest. But their service is not indispensable, while that of the ordained ministry is, if the Church is to remain itself.

On another level, the fact that the ministry is an essential component of the Church cannot derive from the fact that without priests and bishops the Church would be unable to celebrate the Eucharist. This would be a clear *petitio principii*. If we are to take the opposite course, then, we need to inquire into the constitution of the ordained ministry on the level of the existential sacramentality of the Church, that of its existence and its works, what it is and what it does.

3. THE CHARISM OF ORDINATION

Because of the difficulties outlined above, theology today rarely uses priestly terminology to define the ministry; it prefers to work with the basic category of 'sacrament', in the sense of the general sacramentality of the Churcioh. Thinking of the Church as the mystery of the body of Christ made visible in its social framework, it often seems possible to single out the ordained ministry as essentially possessing the visible form that makes Christ operative as head of the body within the overall structure of the ecclesial body. Seen in this way, ordination gives the minister the form of head of the Church, the capacity to act *in persona Christi*, to exercise the vicariate of Christ.

These formulae were used by Vatican II and by the 1971 Synod of Bishops; the form of words used, taken as a whole, however, suffers from an excessive formalism. If there is no specific content attached to the act of ordination (what is one ordained *for?*), then the ministry, in this sort of direct Christological derivation, becomes an impressive but empty form. Too impressive, because it is the form of Christ the head of the whole Church; too empty, because it fails to state how the minister can act as head of the Church; it is thus in danger of being able to embrace and 'Christify' whatever content one cares to give it. Perhaps the concept becomes more plausible if the form of Christ the head is handed down to the ministry not as an immediate result of ordination, but as an attribute of a particular task for which ordination fits ministers. If the tasks derive from the form and not the other way round, pastors become a sort of delegation *ad omnia*, enabled to establish their own competence of themselves, and it would be impossible to establish any set of criteria to determine the degrees and limits of their competence.

The New Testament, which is perhaps almost niggardly in its indications of juridical and sacramental formalities proper to the ministry, is clear enough on the subject of its charism and tasks. The institution of the presbyter-bishops came about because the apostles, before their departure from this world, felt the need to leave the Church an instrument designed to keep unity in fidelity to the teaching which they had received (Acts 20:17-38; Titus 1:5-11; 2 Tim. 2:1-2; 1 Pet. 5:1-4). It is the Word of God that forms the Church and the Holy Spirit who gives it life: the Church therefore lives in a continuous process of lively movement, in a plurality of forms, not in the manner of a synagogue of the law, formed around a document in a rigid institutional form. Yet the apostolic Church can never think of reducing its future to a subjective dispersal of the message in a sort of continual mystic re-invention of its faith. The Church in fact knows itself to be inspired by the Spirit in an infinite multiplicity of forms, but it is equally conscious of being based in its essentials on the witness handed on once and for all by the apostles of the Son of God who came *semel*, once, and was known *semel* in human form. Its foundation on the witness of the apostles is therefore an absolutely essential condition of its unity and of its authenticity. This is why the apostolic Church provides itself with a ministry essential to it, that of presbyter-bishops, whose function is to guarantee its perennial foundation on its one legitimate base.

If the charism of ordination is, then, that of the apostolic foundation of the Church, those who receive the laying-on of hands are destined to the service of the gospel, bound to witness to it in all its purity, placed at the centre of the community as the meeting-point for all other charisms. Their task is not merely to teach a doctrine, but to incarnate the *apostolica vivendi forma* in their own lives. Like an apostle, the ordained minister is called to generate the community through his dedication and, if necessary, sufferings, so that even if a Church can have ten thousand teachers, it can only have one father, recognised as he who dedicates his life to it so it will not lack the vital spark of the teaching of the apostles (see 1 Cor. 4:15). This is why the relationship between the pastor and his flock is unique. His is a position of authority, but authority of a completely new and special kind. The *praesides gentium*, the rules of the gentiles, rule through the force of law and the *imperium*: here however the supreme authority does not reside either in strength or in form, but consists above all in a daily relationship of living and serving. Before the sacred Canons and any other formulation of ecclesiastical discipline, the Church spontaneously grouped and recognised itself round those who through the laying-on of hands had received the gift and duty of basing the Church on the apostles and at the same time reproducing the dedication of the apostles themselves. The supreme authority resides in deeds and derives not from the form of institution but rather from a life's work.

On the other hand, the pastor of the Church has been invested with his task through a sacramental gesture which both signifies and contains the *actio Christi* itself, as a gift of the 'I shall be with you' directed to the purpose for which the sacrament is given. Therefore, where the need for unity in the Church touches on the essential conditions of its apostolicity, the preaching of its ordained ministers becomes a magisterium, which in its highest degree can even be dogmatic and infallible, and their authority takes on well-determined and binding forms. But all this comes about through a process of development proportionate to the need, through a charism and a role experienced basically in the simplicity of daily relationships and the common task of building-up the Christian community.

In a theology of the ministry, it is vital to place the specific content of the charism at the centre. If authority in fact derived not from some specific task but directly from priestly consecration, it would have the dangerous power of rendering all it touched holy and inviolable, to the point where the minister could not be denied the right to burn heretics, as stated in a proposition of Luther's condemned by Leo X ('*Haereticos comburi est contra voluntatem Spiritus*', Dz. 1483). If instead authority is made to derive not from the sacerdotal aspect of ministry but purely from its aspect as sign of Christ the head, it becomes impossible to see where criteria for and limits to its exercise can be drawn from. But if ordination is thought of as the gift of a specific and well-determined charism, the authority of ministry no longer risks being painfully superimposed on other charisms, thereby cancelling out the free and multiform flowering of Christian experience, but can be set at the centre of this experience through the force of apostolic love, becoming an *imperium* only when, and to the extent that this is necessary to guarantee Catholic communion on the basis of the values of apostolic continuity.

The role of the ministry in relation to the Eucharist can also be seen in this way. In the rite of the Eucharist, the Church expresses, *par excellence*, celebrates and nourishes its own priesthood, that priesthood which lives day by day in acts and in faith. In the Eucharist, the priesthood of Christ and of the Church becomes a ritual priesthood; in so far as it relates to Christ it is the source of all the priesthood experienced in the Church through the deeds of its life; in so far as it relates to the Church, it is its summit. Now, if sacraments *significando causant*, cause by signifying, they should be a faithful representation of the priesthood of the Church, which is founded on that of Christ and derived from it. Therefore the Church, which can only reach Christ through the witness of the apostolic tradition, cannot compose a true *repraesentatio* of the mystery it celebrates in its eucharist except by gathering round him who is the servant and the guarantor of its continuity with the apostles. Basically the theology of Ignatius of Antioch concerning the bishop as indis0ensable celebrant of the eucharist is in this line: the apostolic role of the ministry is the basis of its eucharistic role and not *vice versa*. If someone is called on to take the part of Jesus only on the basis of his holiness or the effectiveness of the leadership he actually exercises in the community, this would not be respecting the truth of the mystery, because it is not the human effectiveness of the Church that makes it capable of celebrating the mystery of the body and blood of Christ. But if the call is based only on the fact that he has received sacramental ordination, this would not be respecting the truth of the representation, by which the rite should reproduce the relationship between the Church and Christ, which means that he who breaks the bread should in his turn be someone who serves the Church apostolically and devotes his life to it. This does not mean that a priest who does not in fact serve the community cannot celebrate the Eucharist in it, but only that in this case his figure would not correspond to the basic theological model and would need, in the last resort, to be justified as an affirmation of the transcendence of the sacrament. In the basic theological framework, the Eucharistic role of the priest is founded on his ordination, but in so far as this gives him a charism that places him as the indispensable link in the Church's apostolic tradition.

Furthermore, linking the Eucharistic role directly to the Eucharist produces a sort of sacramental short-circuit that upsets the whole balance of the sacramentality of the Church: each sacrament, in fact, is designed to bring about a grace, that is a new life, and not a second sacrament. If ordination were given for the purpose of celebrating the Eucharist we would have a sacrament that related not just to life and to the priesthood of actions, but to another sacrament. There is no need to think that breaking the ordination-Eucharist short-circuit means losing something of the Catholic dogmatic heritage; on the contrary, it is the only way of recapturing the sense of the absolute novelty of the Christian priesthood as opposed to the priesthood of the Old Law. It also breaks up the formalism of the concept of the vicariate of Christ, through its definition of the content of the charism, and of the precise meaning of the function and position of ordained ministers in the Church. Finally, if the ordained ministry is based on the charism of the apostolic teaching it is freed from the sacral isolation to which the sacerdotal concept had banished it. The ordained ministry still remains at the heart of the Church, as the necessary converging point of all the expressions of its faith, but at the same time it operates on its frontiers, where the apostolic mission continues to tell the world that Jesus is risen and that he is the Lord, where the Church is called to inject the leaven of the gospel into the course of history.

Translated by Paul Burns

Hans Waldenfels

The Right to a Priest?

1. THE PROBLEM

THE QUESTION of the relationship between priest and community allows of three basic options: *Either* priestly existence is thought of without reference to the community, *or* the community is seen independently of its relationship to the priest, *or* the discussion is pursued in the light of the tension which exists between priestly existence and community self-realisation in its various conceptual possibilities. The first option quickly reduces the relationship of priest and community to that of priest and laity, while the second broadens it out to the relationship between the community and its leaders, who no longer need to be priestly leaders. The third option sees the second as endangering a total understanding of community, but it does demand appropriate reflection on the community's self-understanding and consequently a consideration of the relationship between leadership and priesthood.

A. *Priest and laity*

It is possible to conceptualise priesthood in terms of a contradistinction to lay status in the Church. It is then usually linked with the claim to a special 'calling', not from the community, but from God. The genuineness of this is tested by the bishop and his representatives and ratified by the sacramental laying on of hands. In the Church of the Latin rite this is preceded by a period of regulated theological-ascetic training and the affirmation of a binding rule of life. The laying on of hands is given with a view to ministry in the Church, but this no longer has to be a form of ministry which is consciously centred on the community.

So the contrast between 'priest and community' is not to be understood as equivalent to that of 'priest and laity'. The layman himself is primarily a non-priest, who, in particular situations in his religious life, needs priestly intervention. This relationship is, on its part, frequently reduced to the singular relationship 'priest and layman', particularly when, for the individual layman in many cases, it is not the community but only the ordained priest who, as authorised proclaimer and interpreter of the word of God and minister of specific sacraments, can 'help'.

B. *The community and its leader*

This view of things has to be modified in communities where, as a result of both the shortage of available priests as leaders of communities and the number of actual communities, the question of leadership in so-called priestless communities is raised. For the present situation various factors come into play, and these are of great significance:

(i) The community reference in the training of priests has moved in one of two directions. The first is towards the distinct formation of pastoral concern, that is, to caring and tending, the 'cure of souls', and this implies a plurality of mainly individual personal relationships. The other direction is towards missionary concern, that is, to a long period of activity understood as leading towards the forming of a Church. But all this has quite often resulted in the loss of the original relationship between community leadership and the presbyterate. And this separation of priesthood and community leadership in turn renders necessary the authorisation of non-priests for community leadership.

(ii) Experience with communities led by lay-people and the realisation of community within them is partly a result of increasing ecumenical contacts. The rejection of a formerly one-sided sacramentalism and the concentration on the non-sacramental realisation of *marturia, koinonia* and *diakonia* immediately reduce the significance of the presence of the priest as the authorised minister of penance and the Eucharist.

(iii) However, where the central significance of the Eucharist for bringing about the full realisation of community is recognised, it frequently goes hand in hand with emergency solutions for all those exceptional cases where the priestly vocation in the classic, centuries-old style of the Church of the Latin rite no longer suffices. Either reference is made to the high claims which the Church has always made upon the recipient of the Eucharist, or forms of the so-called *missa sicca*, a Eucharistic celebration reduced to the words of institution, have been promulgated, or the faithful, hitherto obliged '*sub gravi*', have abruptly been released from this serious obligation, when attendance at a church for Sunday Mass has been impossible for reasons of distance.

None of the so-called emergency situations, however, are convincing. Thus, interestingly enough, what people have been bound to by the Sunday obligation referred to is not the reception of the Eucharist but participation in the memorial of the death and resurrection of Christ, as this is encountered in the celebration of the gathered community focusing on the repetition of the Eucharistic words of institution at the Last Supper. The distinction between the obligation to receive communion (once a year in the Easter period) and that of participation in the Eucharistic celebration (weekly on Sunday) in the requirement referred to does two things. On the one hand, it supports those who insist on the high claims made upon the recipient of the Eucharist, but, on the other hand, it also contradicts them, if they hold the view that, on the basis of this high claim, allowance can be made for a reduction in the frequency of communion. However, the requirement also opposes those who, on the basis of a renewed understanding of the Eucharist as the sacramental meal for the hungry world, would like to see even more frequent reception of communion ensured, but who also believe that they should forgo the celebration of the memorial of the body given by the Lord as food to his disciples as the basis for the ever new re-presentation and thus the becoming again of the 'body of Christ', which *we* ourselves are and become (see 1 Cor. 10).

C. *Community and priest*

If the concept of priesthood is removed too starkly from community reference, the danger exists that the focus will be directed one-sidedly on the specific individuality of the priest. On the other hand, a concept of community reduced to the reference to a priestly leader stands in danger of allowing the ecclesial reference of all sacramental activities to become blurred, and that includes the celebration of the Eucharist as the fundamental and at the same time the highest way of realising the principle of the gathered community (see *Lumen Gentium* §26).

Every priest is, however, first of all a believer and as such a member of a community. Therefore it is worth considering again the fundamental bond between the priest and the community just as much as the bond between the community and the priest. The question then arises, to what extent does the community need a priest, and when does it have the right to a priest? Answering these questions presupposes the clarification of a number of prior questions. Thus it will be valuable to test what is basically understood by the concept of 'community', which is used as a matter of course so frequently today. What is it that we call community? What are its basic elements, its basic authority? Who establishes these and tests when and where they are to be accepted as given? Is there an extra-community standpoint on the basis of which extra-community authorities can both establish criteria for testing and apply them? Or are already existing communities always those which lay down the conditions for new ones which come into being?

2. 'COMMUNITY'

To answer the questions about 'community' it must be said in advance that two points of departure cannot be played off against each other as mutually exclusive ways of looking. On the one hand, the community cannot be traced back and determined in purely sociological terms, for, on the basis of the Church's self-understanding, the community stands, from a theological point of view, in the tension between the gathering and the sending of those who believe in the word of God. On the other hand, the concrete realisation of community cannot be established and described in purely theological terms, for as a socio-historical entity the community is subject to laws and also to the uncertainties and spontaneities of historical currents and changes.

A. *Theological perplexities*

On the theological level it is accepted that the formation of the community may be described in such phrases as 'gathering under the word of God', 'the proclamation of and witnessing to the gospel in word and deed', 'the coming together of *marturia, koinonia* and *diakonia*' and so on. In the sense of the universal saving claims of Christ, attention must also be paid to the network of local churches in the universal Church, not only in communities of episcopally led local churches but also the structures which unify churches in a common bond to the word of God and also in the mutual bond of the office of teachers, guardians and prophets.

In this sense one may adopt the attempted definition of W. Kasper: 'In a particular place or within a particular circle of people the community is the association, founded through word, sacrament and brotherly service and united by the office of ministry, of those who, in unity with the whole Church, believe in Jesus Christ and bear public witness to this belief. Through one baptism and through common participation at the Lord's table it is one body in Christ. It is sent to allow the love which it has received in Christ to become visible and effective in the world.[1]

However, such a definition says no more in answer to the questions:
> How does a community arise
> When does the process of becoming a community require the realisation of all the elements named here
> Who is the subject of community formation, shaping and realisation
> When and how does the office of ministry become effective
> How often is common participation at the Lord's table to take place?
. . . and many others.

A look at some concrete forms of community realisation may clarify these perplexities for us.

B. *Situations*

Three situations may briefly be sketched as a starting point for further considerations.

Situation I. In many parts of the world today Christian communities are already in existence. The individual believer, because of his own particular circumstances, belongs to a particular parish community in the place where he lives. For its part, the individual community is bound in with a network of parishes, over which episcopal jurisdiction pertains. The episcopal authority decides upon the distribution of the available clergy, the new ordering and establishing of parishes and the amalgamation or abolition of parishes which have grown too small. The parochial principle is determined first of all from the point of view of the overall care of the faithful, secondly from that of the distribution of pastoral resources, primarily on the basis of quantitative considerations, e.g., the number of available priests in relation to that of committed believers. This predominant picture of a territorial network of parish communities is only broken by the subsidiary structures of communities with particular group goals and personnel, e.g., hospital, religious, student, youth and expatriate communities.

Situation II. The community system just described was also the god-parent of those places where, in so-called mission areas previously untouched by Christianity, new communities had first to be founded. The accusation of ecclesiastical colonialism today is aimed precisely at the uncritical transfer of ecclesiastical forms of organisation into the situation of other cultures. It is important to note in this that, at the same time, those who came together in their new-found faith were not subjects, but objects, of the new community foundation. The question arises, however, whether the structures of Church organisation imposed 'from the top' have not contributed to the accusation that Christianity is a foreign, Western, imported religion, and whether they have come to extinguish the initial enthusiasm and fascination of young Christians. The frequent attempts of young churches to free themselves from the influence of Western theology may be regarded here in precisely the same light as the demand made in various Third World countries for a moratorium on the supply of finance and personnel. The conflict which such demands evoke in the Third World itself ought not to obscure the fact that it persists even into that period of drought which people must inevitably go through on their way to achievement of the goal; every true deliverance leads through the desert and awakens debilitating memories of the abundance of the fleshpots of Egypt.

Situation III. This is to be observed today in all places where (*a*) the network of caring no longer functions or is even torn apart, and (*b*) the believers increasingly feel themselves to be no longer the objects of the

Church's care but subjects of the Church's creation of community. In this context mention should be made of 'basic communities', which have been brought more and more into recent discussion, and in the light of which a conscious comparison of differing models is not necessary.

Certainly this may be said: The concept 'basic community' or even 'basic Church community' should not be domesticated by being used for all possible pastoral trivialities, like the district apostolate or certain groups with specific aims in view. It should rather be restricted to the formation of those communities which arise on the basis of their existence as believing communities and the initiative of believing Christians irrespective of their ecclesiastical status—in this sense of 'basic'—and in which consequently a new subject-consciousness on the part of the members of the community is achieved.

Such a process is not vulnerable theologically, since it represents nothing other than the logical outcome of the maturity of the Christian. It is tested without any renewed appeal or new authorisation by the Church's leadership by the extent to which the principle of the gathering and sending of believers in Christ is fulfilled.

However if one starts from the view that the future of the Church, even in those countries in which the communities have existed rather as administrative units than as the living realisation of a community growing to adulthood and maturity in following Christ, lies in the renewal of communities which are growing in Christian maturity, then the awareness of Christians as the subjects of community and the re-allocation of ministries that ensues is the command of the hour everywhere. Such an opinion can be maintained, even if one is concerned about the inclusion of individual communities in the universal Church and on this basis questions the relationship between and the mutual openness of the communities to one another and to their leaders. However this question, in its significance for the way to mutual building up and strengthening of communities in the faith, can only be hinted at here.

3. THE ROLE OF THE PRIEST

The crisis of the caring community—and of the care of the community—the awakening of a new self-awareness in countless numbers of Third World communities, as also in traditionally Christian countries, the experience of communities needing to and being able to manage without a priest—all this leads us back to the question of the role of the priest.[2]

It can be posed independently of whether or not a country has sufficient priests; it simply poses itself with greater emphasis in a period of increasing shortage of priests.

F

Two attitudes appear to come together here. Yet although the priest question is answered in a different way in a community structure stamped by 'caring' ways of thinking from that in a community stamped by ideas of maturity and new self-awareness, both answers proceed on the tacit assumption that a link has existed or exists between the office of community leadership and the priesthood. Only 'caring' ways of thinking work towards a loosening of the link, whereas the other position—if I am judging it correctly—works towards a potentially quite different understanding of this link. But on the answer to this question depends also the answer to the further question, whether and when the community has the right to a priest.

A. *Priest, but not leader?*

Shortage of priests has led to a clear disjunction between leadership and priesthood in many countries. In communities with no pastor, a nun, deacon, catechist, pastoral assistant or other authorised lay-person is entrusted with the leadership of the community. In this way it has been possible to take into account the variety of community tasks to a greater extent than happened in many traditional communities, where the responsibility for everything was laid upon the parish priest. But even if it is right to release the priest from all duties which others may perform as well and even better, it is not right to free him from all functions to such an extent that, ultimately, only the celebration of the mass and the administration of the sacrament of penance remain to him. A one-sided concentration of the priest in the ministry of these sacraments also obscures the fact that the priest is taken from the community and placed there for its benefit, as well as the fact that the sacraments themselves are instituted for the building up of the community.

B. *Leader—and therefore priest*

The fact is, that episcopal laying on of hands places the priest at an intersection. On the one hand, there he remains, subsequently as previously, aligned with that from which he has been taken; from a concrete community for a concrete community. On the other hand, however, he is also included in the fellowship of the presbyterate gathered around the bishop. However, to the extent to which he represents the community, he binds it in his person to the greater community of the local church and, beyond it, the universal Church. This double alignment, however, must remain also constantly represented in the common leadership function in so far as the leader, in a particular sense, is the person who guarantees his own community's openness to and bond with other communities. Herein lies a criterion for the discernment of orthodoxy and orthopraxy. The recently desired emphasis on 'basic *Church* community', in its totality, gains its sense from this bond.

The character of a community which refers beyond itself derives ultimately from its adherence to the word of God and its fulfilment of the demand to follow Christ. To the basic characteristics of the community belong therefore constant listening to the word of God in time and the proclamation and spread of the message in verbal testimony and wordless service to mankind. In this way the community of Christ's followers lives through the constant interaction of gathering in mystical unity and sending to the world outside. However, no-one can deny that life in *'memoria Christi'*, in memory of Christ, and the fulfillment of the demand to gather for the remembrance of the table-fellowship of the Lord's Supper, in order to bring about the sending out to spread the new community of all people in righteousness, peace and the love of Christ, are bound up with the celebration of the Eucharist. The words of the Constitution of the Church, *Lumen Gentium* §26 cannot be ignored: 'In any community existing round an altar, under the sacred ministry of the bishop, there is manifested a symbol of that charity and "unity of the Mystical Body, without which there can be no salvation".' In these communities, though frequently small and poor, or living far from any other, Christ is present. By virtue of Him the one, holy, Catholic and apostolic Church gather together. For 'the partaking of the Body and Blood of Christ, does nothing other than transform us into that which we consume'. What was expressed at the Second Vatican Council has been grasped gratefully again and again since then at Medellin and Puebla. If one starts from the fact that the invitation to the Eucharistic feast in the sense of participation in the Sunday celebration has been newly stated in the Constitution on the Sacred Liturgy of the last Council and has thus received its model there, and if one adds to that, that this feast has not received its valid replacement in a form of receiving communion apart from this celebration, then the Church's credibility is jeopardised when the fulfilment of Christ's command, 'Do this in remembrance of me', is tied, by arbitrary regulations, to conditions which make an appropriate frequency of celebrations impossible.

C. *Consequences*

(i) To the extent to which a community itself becomes the subject of the proclamation of the word, of gathering and sending, it should be able to collaborate in the appointment of a leader as the personality who creates unity and integration; there is no conflict here with the view that leadership is to be seen as a charism or gift of the Spirit.

(ii) Every community leader has need of acceptance and recognition, for the sake of the unity and fellowship of the individual community with the greater Church, by episcopal authority as well as acceptance in the community of leaders.

(iii) Since, however, the Christian community is only established 'when it is rooted and pivoted (*radicem cardinemque!*) in the celebration of the Eucharist' (see *Presbyterorum Ordinis* §6), the identity of the leader and the priest is to be the aim, for he is the legitimate president at the Eucharist and in the firmly established proclamation of the gathering word and the inspiration to various ministries of salvation in the following of Christ.

(iv) In the determination of criteria for acceptance into the presbyterate, notice should be taken first of all of the personal integrity of the candidate's faith and life,[3] and then above all of his suitability for the task of integrating and inspiring as leader of a community.

(v) The training of community leaders should correspond to the level of general as well as of theological education of the believers in a given country or region; to put it another way, differences in level of education and standard of living of the priestly leaders should correspond to the various actual forms within the community, and the scale reaches from the almost completely organised communities in certain Western countries to the hardly noticeable hidden communities on the Chinese mainland.

Translated by Martin Kitchen

Notes

1. W. Kasper *Elemente eine Theologie des gemeinde; Lebendige Seels orge* 27.

2. W. Kasper 'Die Funktion des Priesters in der Kirche' in *Glaube und geshichte* (Mainz 1970) pp. 371-387, especially pp. 379ff.

3. When the well-being of communities in particular countries demands it, there could, in this respect, be no stricter standards applied than in the acceptance of converted Protestant clergy for priestly ministry in Germany.

Norbert Greinacher

The Right of the Parish to a Priest of its Own

1. SOCIOLOGICAL CONSIDERATIONS

FROM the sociological point of view Church communities are to be regarded as secondary groups or voluntary organisations. What characterises primary groups, as for example the family, is that what predominates in them are personal contacts, face-to-face relations, emotional ties, intuition and spontaneity. In secondary groups, on the other hand, social relations are limited to certain dimensions of human life and to certain periods of time. Secondary groups generally concern only certain particular needs, expectations, attitudes and emotions of their members. The secondary group cannot and should not absorb the person totally but instead appeals to and interests only part of his or her life. In this way the secondary group is also oriented towards a particular goal and characterised by a rational organisation.

The local church community as a social group possesses a recognisable identity both for its members and for outsiders too. Like every group, it has a social structure, inasmuch as every member occupies a particular position and thereby also undertakes a particular role in the group. Linked with this is of course the fact that the members are in a situation of comprehensive and mutual communication with each other. As in every group, there are in the Christian community certain norms and models of behaviour which are accepted by its members. Beyond this, the members of a group share common interests, common values, common ideas about the goals of the group's activities. For a group to be able to exist, it must show a certain stability and persistence over the course of time.

For the group to 'function', in other words for it to be able to operate as a group and fulfil its tasks, there are two conditions above all that have to be fulfilled. First, its members have to meet together at regular intervals of time. At these meetings the members can communicate with each other, they can decide which interests are to have priority, conflicts can be settled, tasks can be allotted, agreement can be established, and so on. Secondly, it is necessary that one or more members, depending on the size of the group, be entrusted with the task of leadership: in a democratically run group this is normally for a definite period of time and on the basis of election. This formal ascription of the function of leadership to particular officials in fact differentiates the secondary group yet again from the primary group. The exercise of this function of leadership is of decisive significance for the group's integration, for its effectiveness both internally and externally, in short for its entire life.

2. THEOLOGICAL CONSIDERATIONS

The Church is primarily and essentially realised in the individual local church community. It is significant that when the New Testament speaks of the church what it means is above all the actual coming together of Christians or the particular group of Christians in a particular extended family or in a particular town or city. It is only in relatively few passages that the Church as a whole is meant. This is illuminating when we realise that it is above all in the individual community that the attempt is made to bear witness to the faith, to make love a reality, and to live on the basis of hope. It is in the individual community that by word and symbol the life, death and resurrection of Jesus are recalled, that this remembrance is borne witness to and handed on, and that in his spirit the service of our fellow-men is embodied.

From this point of view the centre of gravity of Church life is to be found not in the Church's central leadership and its ministerial structures but in its embodiment in the individual local community. This latter can be defined as forming a group of people who believe in Jesus Christ and try to make their life both as individuals and as a community conform to the message of the New Testament. Members of the community are tied into it by a network of social relationships and undertake particular functions within it. The focus of the community's life is formed by its assembling together, particularly to celebrate the Eucharist. But the community does not form any kind of ghetto: it sees itself as an integral part of the Church as a whole and is aware of its obligation of service to society at large.

Communities of this kind are formed at the basis of the church and form the basis of the Church. On the one hand, this is to say that these communities have an immediate connection with 'the joys and the hopes, the griefs and the anxieties of the men of this age, especially those who are poor or in any way afflicted'.[1] In the life of these communities, in their meetings and celebrations, in their services and discussions, the history of suffering of their members and of the members of the society in which they live will be articulated, as will also the history of people's love, faith and hope, and the fortunate experiences they have had in their lives. It is through the fact that the members of the community bring to it their individual and collective experiences and interpret them on the basis of their Christian faith that the Church obtains access to human life and from time to time becomes anew a Church of and for mankind. But through this, on the other hand, the communities become the basis of the Church itself. What is demanded of them from outside is not orthodoxy but orthopraxis, the extent to which their actions are fired by and express their faith: the community's experiences inside and outside its own life and its interpretation of these experiences in the light of the Jesus thing become the locus and the context of its orthodoxy.

The living existence of communities of this kind represents the condition for the Church's survival to be possible in a form that corresponds to its understanding of itself. It is only in this way that Christian faith can become relevant in society today, and it is only in this way that this faith can be handed on to the rising generation.

Communities of the kind we are talking about will exist in many varied and different forms. It would be completely wrong to assume that we could hit on a uniform pattern of community life. But this means that we return to a situation that we already meet with in the New Testament. Such communities can for example be of a non-territorial kind, as for example a university parish, a religious community, a parish confined to a linguistic minority. Such communities can also arise by the emergence of a network of subsidiary structures within a large city parish. They can be formed at the level of former small parishes, now merged in larger structures, in country districts. They can develop as a kind of core community at the level of an existing parish. They can be established as *communautés de base*, basic communities, perhaps at a critical distance from the official Church hierarchy and sometimes also marked by a definite political stance.

The celebration of the Eucharist is of central importance for the community's identity. In agreement with the statements of the New Testament and the Church's oldest traditions, the Second Vatican Council lays down that the celebration of the Eucharist 'contains the Church's entire spiritual wealth' and is 'the source and the apex of the whole work of preaching the gospel',[2] indeed 'the fount and apex of the whole Christian life'.[3] The Council calls on pastors to 'arrange for the celebration of the Eucharistic sacrifice to be the centre and culmination of the whole life of the Christian community'.[4] And in another place it states that the Church 'constantly lives and grows' from the Eucharist.[5]

Good leadership is moreover of decisive importance for the community's life. The person who undertakes the ministry of leadership in the community is the person who is officially entrusted with this task, in other words the person ordained by the bishop in order that the unity of the community and the unity of the Church is realised. He will try to create as much communication as possible within the community, to offer opportunities for discussion and debate, to provide an institutional structure for dialogue. If conflicts arise, it will be up to him above all to solve them in a Christian way. His task is above all to establish peace, to bring about reconciliation, without masking the points of difference. The ordained leader of the community has further the task of promoting inter-communication in the context of the Church as a whole, both with the diocesan church and with neighbouring communities. He must be particularly aware of his responsibility for seeing that his community does not become a sect that shuts itself in on itself but that it sees and understands itself as part of the Church as a whole. In this connection the individual community must always be open to critical questioning on the part of the universal Church. Another thing that falls to the ordained leader of the community is official concern for the continuity of the Jesus thing. He must be particularly concerned for maintaining coherence with the apostolic traditions. In the fulfilment of this task it is possible for him occasionally to adopt a critical stance over against the community and criticise certain activities, perhaps also certain individuals, to adopt a prophetic role and exhort the community to mend its ways. In this connection the leader of the community has of course to an especial extent the official task of bearing public witness to the Jesus thing. He must see to it that this is handed on to the next generation. And it is particularly his responsibility to see to it that Christian faith is present in our society as a real option.

Now it is precisely if one wants to integrate the celebration of the sacraments into the whole life of the Christian community, if one sees the sacraments above all as the articulation of the life of the community, as the sign of its faith and that of the individual Christian, it is precisely in this case that one must be in favour of the Church clinging on to its old tradition and refusing to separate the ministry of leading the community from that of presiding at the celebration of the Eucharist.

If one takes as one's starting point the central importance of the celebration of the Eucharist for the Christian community, then it is quite nonsensical to separate the task of presiding at the celebration of this 'apex of the whole Christian life' from that of leading the community. This would mean dangerously separating the celebration of the Eucharist from the rest of the life of the community and forcing the priest into the disastrous role of purely a 'massing priest'. With Karl Rahner we must without qualification 'stick firmly to the principle that the ordained leader of the Eucharistic celebration and the community leader as such have to be one and the same person and therefore the former cannot simply be a subordinate functionary for liturgical acts in the congregation. . . . The theory that the leader of the Eucharistic celebration and the community leader need not, or even should not, in principle be identical leads in practice to the eventual decline of the community and to an unchristian neglect of the sacramental element in the Church'.[6]

3. THE WORLD-WIDE SHORTAGE OF PRIESTS

In sharp contradiction to the demand that every local church community should be led by a priest of its own is the world-wide shortage of priests. The total number of all priests, both secular and regular, which still amounted to 420,429 in 1971, dropped to 404,783 in 1975, although the total number of Catholics had increased from 669 million to 717 million over the same period.[7] There are admittedly some exceptions throughout the world to this fall in the number of priests, as for example Poland, Slovenia, the Philippines, parts of Mexico and some dioceses in the USA. But on the whole all the signs point to the fact that, given the same structure and conditions, what we have to deal with is an irreversible process that in its range and extent threatens the existence and survival of the Church. A few examples may help to make this clear.

In West Germany the number of secular and regular priests engaged in normal parish work dropped from 15,546 in 1950 to 13,253 in 1975. The proportion of Catholics to every priest rose over the same period from 879 to 1,084.[8] The number of ordinations to the secular priesthood dropped from 504 in 1962 to 163 in 1978.[9] In Austria the number of ordinations to both the secular and regular priesthood fell from 153 in 1967 to 62 in 1976.[10] In Spain 825 priests were still being ordained in the year 1961-62, but by 1974-75 the number had dropped to only 231.[11]

The consequences brought about by this catastrophic shortage of priests have been shown in an exemplary manner by the study carried out in the Austrian diocese of Gurk (Klagenfurt) by K. Pirker. He demonstrated that in parishes with a priest mass-attendance averaged 48 per cent but in the parishes without a priest it was only 30 per cent.[12] Similar findings are shown in the case of other indicators of church life.

With regard to this state of affairs we must take note of the fact that throughout the world there are very many local church communities which do not have an ordained leader of their own. But it cannot be emphasised clearly enough that for sociological and theological reasons a community without a priest is in principle a nonsense and that every possible effort must be made to overcome this disastrous state of affairs. The joint synod of the dioceses of the German Federal Republic was right to state: 'The Christian community finds its highest realisation in the celebration of the Eucharist. Since the sacrament of unity is not possible without the priestly ministry of unity, there can in the proper sense of the word be no such thing as a community without a priest.[13] The installation of non-ordained women and men as what are termed 'non-ordained reference persons'—a term which anyway is a contradiction in itself—can therefore only be regarded as an emergency solution. Naturally this applies too with regard to deacons.

In addition, 'celebrations of communion' or 'services of the Word concluding with the distribution of communion' held without a priest are to be rejected on theological grounds. It has admittedly been shown that priestless makeshift services of this kind did already exist in previous centuries.[14] But, as A. Schilson has convincingly demonstrated, priestless communion services of this kind on the one hand diminish the significance of the liturgy of the Word, a liturgy which is important for theological and pastoral reasons, while on the other hand they obstruct the way towards a comprehensive understanding of the celebration of the Eucharist as a memorial celebration, set in the context of a meal, of the death and resurrection of Jesus Christ.[15]

Of recent years the impression of a certain double standard has been difficult to resist when on the one hand prelates continue in traditional fashion to underline Catholics' serious obligation to attend Mass on Sunday, while on the other there is a playing down of the significance of the celebration of the Eucharist for the life of a community presided over by its ordained leader. Here what is at stake is the credibility of the hierarchy.

4. EVERY COMMUNITY WITH ITS OWN PRIEST

If in the Church there are anything like regular laws which are immune to human interference in all different historical and social contexts because they result from the situation itself, from the statements of the New Testament and from the continuous traditions of the Church, then one example is the 'right of the community to its priest'.[16] The joint synod of the dioceses of the German Federal Republic states that 'according to the oldest tradition of the Church it is the right and duty of Christian people to come together on the Lord's day for the Eucharist'.[17]

The paradoxical aspect of this situation consists in the fact that in the Church today there is in most countries no lack of vocations to the priestly ministry. The steeply rising number of theology students in West Germany is just as much an index of this as is the large number of catechists and non-ordained leaders of *communautés de base* throughout the world, quite apart from the number of women who are willing and able, to say nothing of married priests. What is becoming more and more obvious is that obligatory celibacy may not be the only but is certainly the decisive obstacle to the granting of the local church community's right to its own priest. With regard to this dilemma Karl Rahner has taken a clear stand: 'If the Church in a concrete situation cannot find a sufficient number of priestly congregational leaders who are bound to celibacy, it is obvious and requires no further theological discussion that the obligation of celibacy must not be imposed.'[18] The 1972 Swiss synod stated that new forms of the priestly ministry must be recognised. In a request to the Vatican Congregation for the Clergy the Brazilian bishops pointed to the enormous shortage of priests in their country and advocated the ordination of married men to the priesthood.[19] The diocesan synod of Durban, South Africa, came out in favour of the admission of married men to the priesthood. The first national convention of the Catholic Church in the USA advocated scrapping the obligation of celibacy for secular priests. A joint working party of the English and Welsh bishops' conference and the national conference of priests regarded the possibility of married priests as an absolute pastoral necessity. The bishops of central France referred to the serious crisis of vocations to the priesthood during their *ad limina* visit to the pope in March 1977.

It is continually becoming clearer that those who are conservative in the original sense of the word are those who want to cling on to what is understood to be the primary tradition of the community's right to a priest of its own, even if this means renouncing the secondary tradition of obligatory celibacy, while those who by their insistence on obligatory celibacy refuse local communities this right are making radical changes in the Church's situation. Heretical structures are emerging in the Church under our very eyes inasmuch as the actual leadership of the community is kept separate from ordination and communities are deprived of the Sunday celebration of the Eucharist. While in the entire tradition of the Church the participation of all Christians in the same Eucharistic bread has been valued as a sign of the communion of saints, today an ever larger number of communities are in fact 'excommunicated'. Nobody should be amazed if the refusal of the right to an ordained leader of the community leads to an 'underground Church' in which non-ordained Christians take over the job of presiding at the Eucharist. This, however, threatens the unity of the Church.

In this connection it goes without saying that in the future not every ordained leader of a local Christian community can be a priest with an academic education and giving his whole time to his ministry. In the future the priestly ministry will take on a very wide variety of forms.

Besides the man with an academic education will be the priest who has gained his theological and spiritual competence by another route. There will be those whose ministry is a full-time occupation and those who can only devote their spare time to it while earning their living in a full-time job, there will be honorary priests, there will be married priests alongside unmarried ones. There are also no theological reasons to be found why the priestly ministry should not also be entrusted to women and why it cannot be exercised for only a limited period. Moreover, the priestly ministry of leadership will be more closely tied in with the structures of the community than before and shared in by committees. If the Church opens up access to the priestly ministry in this way, then every local Church community will be able to be granted its right to an ordained leader and to its own Sunday celebration of the Eucharist.

Translated by Robert Nowell

Notes

1. The opening words of the pastoral constitution on the Church in the modern world. This and other Council documents are cited from the translation edited by Walter M. Abbott, S.J. *The Documents of Vatican II* (London and Dublin 1966).
2. Decree on the Ministry and Life of Priests, section 5.
3. Dogmatic Constitution on the Church, section 11.
4. Decree on the Bishops' Pastoral Office in the Church, section 30:2.
5. Dogmatic Constitution on the Church, section 26.
6. Karl Rahner *The Shape of the Church to Come* (London 1974) pp. 111-112.
7. *Annuarium statisticum Ecclesiae* 1971 and 1975.
8. *Kirchliches Handbuch* (Cologne 1977) XXVIII.
9. *Zur Pastoral der geistlichen Berufe* (1979) XVII p. 11.
10. F. Klostermann *Wir brauchen Priester* (Linz n.d.) p. 12.
11. *Ibid.,* p. 48.
12. As far as I know the report of this investigation has not been published. I am relying on P. M. Zulehner 'Der Priestermangel und seine Folgen' in F. Klostermann (ed.) *Der Priestermangel und seine Konsequenzen* (Düsseldorf 1977) pp. 11-26: the reference here is to pp. 16-17.
13. From the synod document on the pastoral ministries in the community, 2:5:3, to be found in the official complete edition of the *Gemeinsame Synode der*

Bistümer in der Bundesrepublik Deutschland (Frieburg-im-Breisgau 1976) I p. 608.

14. A. Heinz 'Ersatzgottesdienste für die Sonntagsmesse: Beispiele aus der Geschichte zu einer aktuellen Problematik' in *Trierer theologische Zeitschrift* 86 (1977) pp. 11-24.

15. A. Schilson 'Ein Schritt in die falsche Richtung: kritische Bemerkung zur gegenwärtigen Praxis sonntäglicher Kommunionfeiern' in *Diakonia* 9 (1978) pp. 62-67.

16. This was in fact the title of a leading article written jointly by the editorial staff of the magazine *Diakonia* 8 (1977) pp. 217-221.

17. The synod document on pastoral ministries in the community 5:3:4, cited in n. 13 above p. 624.

18. Karl Rahner *The Shape of the Church to Come* p. 110.

19. For this and what follows, see F. Klostermann *Wir brauchen Priester* (Linz n.d.).

Hans-Jürgen Vogels

The Community's Right to a Priest in Collision with Compulsory Celibacy

A.

FROM what is at first a practical point of view, the present pastoral situation in many countries presents the following problem: Does not the right of communities to the celebration of the Eucharist, and so to a priest, take precedence over the Church law of compulsory celibacy when the effect of this law is that a sufficient number of priests is no longer available?[1] By virtue of the principle that sacraments are necessary to salvation,[2] and in view of the fact that the celebration of the Eucharist is essential to a Christian community (Acts 2:42, 46; Heb. 10:25 etc.), and by virtue of the apostle Paul's ordination rule ('appoint elders in every town', Titus 1:5; and see Acts 14:23), the community's right to a priest must be based in divine law, that is, willed by God, since 'the salvation of souls is the highest law'.[3] On the other hand, the law of celibacy of the Latin Church in the West is generally recognised to be based merely in ecclesiastical, not in divine, law.[4] Where the divine right of the communities and the ecclesiastical obligation on priests collide, the solution of the conflict must, therefore, be automatic: the ecclesiastical obligation ought to give way to the divinely granted right.

B.

The more serious theological reasons for the increasing refusal of a sufficient number of clerical students and priests to submit to the law of obligatory celibacy are overwhelmingly the result of the internal contradictions of this law. The very fact that it appears to conflict with a

84

divine law makes it seem inherently dubious. It is these contradictions in the law—not in celibacy as a freely chosen evangelical way of life for priests and lay-people—which are the subject of this article.

1. THE EXEGETICAL DATA

(a) The saying of Jesus which deals explicitly with celibacy, Matt. 19:10-12, shows, on a more accurate exegesis,[5] that it is impossible to make celibacy a legal requirement. Jesus is here not so much imparting advice as describing the conditions under which a person can choose celibacy: 'Not all can grasp this thing (not marrying), but only those to whom it is given' (Matt. 19:11). The results of the discussion on this saying of Jesus can be briefly summarised as follows. In the final version of Matthew, which alone counts as the word of God,[6] it is prompted by the disciples' disappointment at Jesus' strict requirement of the indissolubility of marriage (Matt. 19:1-9): 'If the position between man and wife is such (that divorce is impossible), it is not advisable to marry' (Matt. 19:10). The disciples are looking for an escape in not marrying at all. Jesus denies them this escape with the remark, 'Not all can grasp this thing'. 'Grasp' (RSV 'receive', *chōrein*) means, not, as used to be argued, 'understand'—which would be expressed in the New Testament by *gnōnai, sunienai, noein*, as in Matt. 13:11, according to which knowledge of the secrets of the kingdom of heaven has already been given to the disciples—but 'find room for'.[7] What is meant is thus not intellectual capacity, but the physical-psychological, total human capacity to undertake celibacy. According to Jesus' words it is a 'thing (*logos, dabar, debirah*, i.e., word and thing) which is not given (*dedotai*) to all'. In Jesus' language the passive expresses an act of God.[8] The capacity to cope with celibacy is therefore a particular gift of God.

Moreover, it is a gift which has already been given: '*hois dedotai*, to those to whom it is given' (perfect), not 'to whom it will be given' (future) as, for example, in James 1:5: 'If any of you lacks wisdom, let him ask . . . and it will be given him (*dothēsetai*).' In Matt. 19:11 there is no call to pray for the gift of celibacy, but a warning against choosing celibacy without the relevant gift. Corresponding to the perfect 'is given' or not, we have in the immediately following explanation in Matt. 19:12: 'For there *are* eunuchs who have been born incapable of marriage, eunuchs who have been made incapable of marriage by men, and there are eunuchs who have made themselves incapable of marriage for the sake of the kingdom of heaven.' In all three cases the reference is to a pre-existing incapacity for marriage, otherwise Jesus would not have listed them in parallel: two are natural and one is God-given. The only possible attitude is therefore to recognise and accept the gift (to castrate oneself spiritually), to assent to the gift and collaborate with it, but not to pray for it—otherwise Jesus would surely have called for prayer. In fact, he calls at the end for those who have received the gift to use it: 'Whoever can grasp it (i.e., whoever *has* the capacity for it), let him grasp it' (Matt. 19:12d). We must, then, recognise the 'diversity of gifts' (1 Cor. 12:4): 'Not all' have received the charism of celibacy.

(b) Paul expresses a similar view on celibacy in 1 Cor. 7:7: 'I would like everyone to be as I am (i.e., celibate), but each has (*echei*) his own spiritual gift (*charisma*) from God, one of one kind and one of another.' Paul's wish that all should be celibate fails in the face of diversity of the gifts Christians have received from God. And Corinthians, like Matthew, presents this supernatural gift as already given: 'Each has (present referring to a state) his own spiritual gift.' If this state could be changed in any way, by prayer, for example, Paul's wish would be capable of fulfilment and he would not have written his great But (*alla*), but called for prayer, as in 1 Cor. 12:31, with reference to other spiritual gifts: 'Earnestly desire the higher gifts' (RSV). Here he does not do that. The 'charism' of celibacy (and now the name appears openly) is already given, and can only be recognised and not prayed for. It is true that Gal. 5:23 describes continence (*enkrateia*) as a fruit of the Spirit which can be obtained by prayer, but this is also necessary at times for married people (1 Cor. 7:5; Titus 1:8), and not to be equated with celibacy as a way of life for the sake of the kingdom, which includes giving up the goods of marriage and family.

It thus appears from Matt. 19:11-12 and 1 Cor. 7:7 that celibacy for the sake of the kingdom of heaven does not depend on the free choice of Christians, but is a gift of God which is not given to all.

(c) Another scriptural text which is of immense importance for evaluating the law of celibacy is 1 Cor. 9:5.[9] In Chapter 9 Paul is talking about his rights as an apostle, rights he enjoys in common with the other apostles, even if he does not make use of them. The rights in question are not just the right to be supported by the Church (1 Cor. 9:4), in terms of the Lord's injunction, 'Eat and drink what they provide, for the labourer deserves his wages' (Luke 10:7-8). Paul is also thinking of the right to be accompanied by a wife: 'Do we not have the right to be accompanied by a sister as wife, as the other apostles and the brothers of the Lord and Cephas?' (1 Cor. 9:5).

This *right*, no less than the other, derives from the *Lord*, that is, it is *ius divinum*, since no other authority than the Lord could grant the apostles an apostolic right. The context also shows this. 9:1 says, 'Am I not free? Am I not an apostle? Have I not seen Jesus our *Lord*?', and at the end there is a recapitulation: 'In the same way, the Lord commanded that those who proclaim the gospel should live by the gospel' (9:14).

The content of the right referred to in 9:5 is that the apostle may be accompanied by a *wife*. This is proved by fact, tradition and language. The proof from fact: Peter-Cephas was married, according to Mark 1:30, which mentions his mother-in-law, whom Jesus cured. According to Eusebius (*Ecclesiastical History* III. 20, 1-5) the brother of the Lord Judas-Thaddaeus was married, since he had two grandsons; similarly, according to the same work (III. 31, 2-3), the apostle Philip, who had three daughters. From 1 Cor. 9:5 we learn that the apostles at a later period were once more being accompanied by their wives on missionary journeys, although in Jesus' lifetime they 'had left all and followed him' (Matt. 19:27). The companion of an apostle can have been no-one but a wife since then, as now, any other companion (if the apostles were married) would only have aroused suspicion. In particular, no other woman could have been the object of a 'right' enjoyed by the apostles. Only marriage gives a man a right to a woman. There is no right to a female servant, even for an apostle, for the Lord says, 'The Son of man came not to be served but to serve'(Mark 10:45 parr) and 'the disciple' of Jesus, the apostle, is in this regard not 'above his master' (Matt. 10:24 par.).[10] Marriage is here included among the special rights of an apostle not only because wives helped apostles in the preaching of the gospel, but also because apostles could claim maintenance from the communities— the 'food and drink' of v. 4—for their wives as well as themselves. In itself, however, marriage in the bible is a general natural law: 'It is not good that the man should be alone. Let us make him a helper fit for him' (Gen. 2:18, 24; Matt. 19:4-6), and Paul has spoken in detail about this right only a few chapters earlier: 'Because of the danger of unchastity, each man should have his own wife.' (1 Cor. 7:2; and see 9:28, 36). Since the basic right was established, Paul did not need to elaborate on it in Chapter 9.

The proof from tradition. The oldest Fathers of the Church translate, without exception, the Greek *gunaikas* by *uxores*, 'wives'. Contrary views appear only in a later period. Tertullian writes around 204 in *De exh. cast.* 8:[11] 'The apostles also were allowed to marry and be accompanied by wives' (1 Cor. 9:5), though he later changed his view under the influence of Montanism.[12] Clement, in *Paedagogus* II. 1, 9,[13] refers to 'being accompanied by wives', as, like 'food and drink' in 9:4, a morally indifferent and so permitted 'use' of creation. Hilary of Poitiers (d. 367), in his commentary on the psalms,[14] interprets the verse in a similar way to Tertullian. It affirms, he says, the 'right of the apostles to marry (not merely to remain married if they had been married before their call): 'Though he praises continence, the apostle does not oppose the right to marry: . . . Do we not have the right to be accompanied by a wife . . . (1 Cor. 9:5)?' Hilary is a doctor of the Church,[15] not merely a Church father, and so his word has great weight. Finally, as late as 383, both Jerome and

G

his opponent in *Adv. Helvidium* 11 translate *uxores circumducere*, 'to be accompanied by wives'.[16] Ten years later Jerome is already under the influence of the Latin celibacy regulations and, in *Adv. Jovinianum* 1. 26 (around 393),[18] translates *mulieres*. They were, he says, women 'who gave them assistance out of their wealth, in . . . the same way that the Lord received assistance' (Luke 8:1-2). Subsequent exegesis has followed Jerome through this escape hatch.

Finally, linguistically, it is a rule that a woman who stands to a man grammatically in a relation analogous to possession is always his wife (e.g., 1 Cor. 7:2, 'have his own wife'. The Greek word is *gunē*, which may mean 'woman' or 'wife' according to the context). The 'accompanying women' of 1 Cor. 9:5 are therefore, according to New Testament usage, the apostles' wives.[19] If, therefore, the apostles enjoyed a biblical right to be accompanied by wives, a right which they could, but were not required to, forgo, the ecclesiastical prohibition on the marriage of priests (Can. 132, 1072 CIC) stands on feet of clay, since priests are successors of the apostles and have taken over their duties and rights.

(*d*) There can be no doubt about the qualifications required for the office of priest, which are set out in 1 Tim. 3:2 and Titus 1:6: 'The priest must be blameless, the husband of one wife.' If he was supposed to have been only once married, then he was certainly allowed to be married.

Since this is an apostolic right, rooted in scripture, and has been preserved by the Eastern Church down to the present, the Latin particular law, in so far as it admits no married man to the priesthood, is not apostolic, and it may be asked whether it has any right to exist in the 'Catholic and apostolic Church' since it is in conflict with its origins.

(*e*) This view is reinforced by 1 Tim. 4:1-5, in which we are told that the Holy Spirit prophesies that to 'forbid marriage' will be a 'later' prompting of 'deceitful spirits and doctrines of demons'. In truth, we are told, 'everything created by God is good, and nothing is to be rejected if it is received with thanksgiving; for then it is consecrated by the word of God and prayer'. Now we shall be showing that compulsory celibacy originated as a prohibition of marriage and, according to Canon 132, still is such. As a prohibition, however, it conflicts with the dogma, the official doctrine of the Catholic Church, that creation is good and marriage is therefore not to be forbidden. Voluntary continence, according to 1 Cor. 7:25-40, is something else. It is 'no command' (7:25), nor ought it to be 'a restraint' (7:35). Humility requires us to recognise that error in disciplinary matters is possible even in the Latin Church, since it is infallible only in faith.[20]

2. HISTORICAL DEVELOPMENT

(*a*) In the first three centuries we hear nothing of the obligation of priestly celibacy.[21]

(b) The first reasons, put forward in the fourth century, for the prohibition on begetting children within a valid priestly marriage are clearly hostile to the body and to marriage. Unless Canon 33 of the Synod of Elvira (around 304) is to be interpreted in the opposite sense as a prohibition on continence,[22] this was the first council (otherwise it was Ancyra in 314) to forbid the continuation of marriage after ordination: 'It was agreed completely to forbid . . . priests: (they are) to be continent and not to beget children.' (the text is contradictory).[23] While no reason is given, the prohibition in itself already falls under the ban of 1 Tim. 4:2-3. The prohibition on having children issued by Pope Siricius in a letter to Himerius of Tarragona (10 February 385)[24] does, however, clearly contain a reason: it is a 'crime, to beget children long after ordination' even 'with one's own wife'. 'All priests and levites are bound by an irrevocable law to consecrate both their hearts and their bodies to chastity from the day of ordination onwards.' The act of procreation is here declared to be unchaste, and those who ignore the prohibition are to be expelled from the priesthood and nevermore to be able 'to celebrate the sacred mysteries of which they have deprived themselves by following *obscene desires*'. That this is a condemnation of the creative work of marriage is plain. From a present-day point of view this law can no longer claim any validity because it is open to dogmatic challenge in its justification and, moreover, interfered in the essential elements of marriage, which is guaranteed by divine law, by seeking to deprive priests of 'the right over their bodies with regard to those acts connected with the production of children' (the modern Canon 1013 section 2 CIC). But Church law cannot cancel divine law.

(c) Similarly open to challenge is the justification—there was only one!—given by the Second Lateran Council for making priestly ordination a bar to marriage. This is the decisive and so far definitive formulation of the law of celibacy and has remained to this day, not a principle of selection, but an absolute bar to marriage! The council declares marriages of priests already contracted or to be contracted in the future invalid, 'so that the law of continence and that purity which is pleasing to God may spread among ecclesiastical persons. . . .'[25] If the purity which is pleasing to God can be achieved only outside marriage, the council is saying: indirectly that the marital union is impure, which, of course, was the teaching of medieval theology.[26] However, by so doing the council contradicted its own teaching on the sacramentality of marriage: 'Those who, under the pretence of piety, condemn the sacraments of the Eucharist, infant baptism, priestly ordination and lawful marriage, we reject as heretics.'[27] The law of 1139 also conflicts with both dogma and divine law by dissolving marriages hitherto regarded as valid, in contravention of Matt. 19:6: 'What God has joined together, let not man put asunder' (RSV), and in addition completely depriving priests of the divine right to marriage (see above 1 (c)). But an *ecclesiastica regula*, which is how the celibacy law of 1139 describes itself, can never invalidate divine law (see Can. 6, no 6 CIC), since divine law is superior.[28] Accordingly the law of 1139, like that of 385, must be regarded as invalid.

(d) The Council of Trent made no new law, but merely confirmed the existing one.[29] It was defended against the Reformers with the remark, 'God will give the gift of chastity to those who ask him for it in the proper way,'[30] which seems to contradict the New Testament evidence (1 (a) (b) above).

(e) The 1918 Code of Canon Law also fails to consider that for celibacy a charism is required which, according to Matt. 19:11, 'not all' have; it rules that clerics in 'major orders are *prevented* from marrying' (Can. 132) and that an 'attempt at marriage' is 'invalid' (Can. 1072). This is the old prohibition on marriage of 1139, one of the 'obligations' (CIC II. 1, 3) imposed by law on priests, not a principle of selection for those who have received the charism of celibacy. The prohibition of marriage falls under the judgment of 1 Tim. 4:3, that it is inspired, not by the Holy Spirit, but by demons. The affirmation of free will introduced in 1930 made no difference to this, since it concerned, not the charism, but only obedience to the law.[31] A law unjustified in itself cannot be legitimised even by voluntary obedience.

(f) The Second Vatican Council for the first time stressed the necessity of the charism, but at the same time 'confirmed' the 'law' which 'imposed' celibacy on all who were to be ordained.[32] The council thereby forced all priests to keep the law, if necessary without the charism, which, according to Matt. 19:11 and 1 Cor. 7:7, is not possible (1 (a) (b) above) or, alternatively, it wants, in the face of the New Testament statements that God calls married people to the priesthood (1 (c) (d) above), to compel God by a law to give all priests the charism of celibacy. God, however, who 'apportions to each one individually as he wills', (1 Cor. 12:11 RSV), cannot be compelled, even by prayer, for which the council calls,[33] particularly since the possibility of obtaining the charism by prayer is very doubtful (1 (a) (b)).

CONCLUSION

Today we have a worldwide shortage of priests and a greater awareness of human rights, including those of priests, who, of course, in the Eastern Roman Catholic Church may be married. In addition to this contradiction, the law of celibacy is internally contradictory. It therefore seems time to recognise that the gift of celibacy is not at our disposal (1 (a) (b)) and to restore to priests in the Western Catholic Church the divine and apostolic right to be accompanied by a wife (1 (c)). This would open a vast dimension for the praise of God and Christ, who poured out all the sacraments, marriage as well as the Eucharist and the priesthood, from his pierced side.[34]

Translated by Francis McDonagh

Notes

1. Karl Rahner 'Pastorale Dienste und Gemeindeleitung' *Stimmen der Zeit* 195 (1977) 742; *Das Recht der Gemeinde auf Eucharistie,* published by the Diocese of Speyer Catholic Priests' Solidarity Group, with essays by Josef Blank, Peter Hünermann and Paul M. Zulehner (Trier 1978) pp. 25-26.

2. Denzinger-Schönmetzer *Enchiridion Symbolorum* 1604. Subsequently cited as DS.

3. B. Häring *The Law of Christ* I (Slough 1978).

4. K. Mösdorf *Kirchenrecht* I (Paderborn, 11th ed. 1964) pp. 261-262.

5. J. Blinzler 'Εἰσὶν εὐνοῦχοι. Zur Auslegung von Matt. 19:12' ZNW 48 (1957) 254-270; H. Baltensweiler 'Die Ehe im Neuen Testament' AThANT 52 (Zurich-Stuttgart 1967) 102-112; H.-J. Vogels *Pflichtzölibat. Eine kritische Untersuchung* (Munich 1978) pp. 21-35. (Unless otherwise indicated, biblical quotations are translated from the author's German.)

6. DS 1501, 3006; Vatican II *Dei Verbum* 1.

7. Liddell and Scott *A Greek-English Lexicon* (Oxford, 6th ed. 1966) p. 2015. According to W. Gesenius (*Hebräische und aramäisches Wörterbuch über das Alte Testament* 17th ed. (Leipzig 1915-1959), the Aramaic parallel terms to *chōrein* given in Hatch and Redpath *Concordance to the Septuagint* II (Oxford 1897) p. 1482, *hazak, jakal, kul, naśa* and *kᵉbet,* never mean intellectual apprehension but spatial absorption.

8. See J. Jeremias *The Eucharistic Words of Jesus* (London 1966).

9. J. B. Bauer 'Uxores circumducere (1 Cor. 9:5)' BZ NF 3 (1959) 94-102; H.-D. Wendland *Die Briefe an die Korinther Neues Testament Deutsch* 12th ed. (Göttingen 1968) VII p. 71; Vogels *Pflichtzölibat* pp. 69-86.

10. See G. Theissen 'Soziologie der Jesus-Bewegung' *Theologische Existenz heute* 194 (Munich 1977, 2nd ed. 1978), 28ff.

11. *Corpus Christianorum* II, 1026-1027. 'Licebat et apostolis nubere et uxores circumducere'.

12. *De monog.* 8.6 (*Corpus Chr.* II, 1239-1240).

13. PG 8, 392B; See 1156-1157.

14. CSEL 22, 483, 8-17: 'apostolus, cum continentiam laudat, non inhibet iam potestatem nubendi . . .: numquid non habemus potestatem mulieres circumducendi . . .?'

15. LThK 5, 337.

16. PL 23, 194B (204A).

17. See *infra* 2b.

18. PL 23, 245B (257A).

19. H.-J. Vogels 'O sentido de 1 Corintios 9:5' *Actualidades Biblicas* (Sao Paulo 1971) 558-571. Reviewed: *Eph. Carm.* 12 (1961) 476ff.

20. Ignorance of such general principles of construction as 'Particularia generalikus non derogont' is one thing, ignorance of major pronouncements of councils and popes is another: the definition of papal infallibility by Pope Pius IX at Vatican I twice explicitly referred to teaching in faith *or* morals (*doctrina(m) de fide vel moribus*) (DS 3074). (Editor's note.)

21. The *Acta martyrum* of Abitine (203) record a priest and his sons among the martyrs; G. Denzler *Das Papsttum und das Amtszölibat* I (Stuttgart 1973) pp. 5-7.

22. See M. Meigne 'Concile ou Collection d'Elvire?' RHE 70 (1975) pp. 361-387.

23. DS 117: 'Placuit in totum prohibere episcopis, presbyteris et diaconibus . . . abstinere se a coniugibus et non generare filios.'

24. DS 185, and a fuller version (retaining some extreme language) in editions of Denzinger up to 32.

25. *Conc. Oec. Decr.*, 3rd ed. (Bologna 1973) p. 198.

26. See M. Müller *Die Lehre des hl. Augustinus von der Paradiesesehe und ihre Auswirkung in der Sexualethik des 12. and 13. Jahrhunderts bis Thomas von Aquin* (Regensburg 1954) 279: 'no conception without sin'.

27. DS 718; LThK 3, 681.

28. A. van Hove *Commentarium Lovaniense in Codicem Iuris Canonici* I, 1. Prolegomena, 2nd ed. (Malines-Rome 1945) p. 51: 'Nullum ius humanum contra ius divinum praevalet.'

29. DS 1809.

30. E. Schillebeeckx *Clerical Celibacy Under Fire* (London 1968) 39 n. 3; Vogels *Pflichtzölibat* 47ff.

31. *AAS* 23 (1931) p. 127. Pope Paul VI ordered a public consecration, and he too referred, not to a charism, but only to an *obligatio*: *AAS* 64 (1972) 539.

32. *Presbyterum Ordinis* 16; *LThK Konzil* 3, 216, 221.

33. *LThK Konzil* 3, 221; see *supra* n. 28.

34. DS 1529, 1600, 1799.

PART IV

Towards an Overall Evaluation

Edward Schillebeeckx

The Christian Community and its Office-Bearers

THIS problem is sufficiently clearly outlined in the editoral of this number of *Concilium*. We have therefore no need to retun to it here, but will confine ourselves, in this concluding article, to a synthesis and to the question of the Christian community and its office-bearers. In it, we shall reflect critically and theologically about the shortage of priests in the light of the community's apostolic right to office-bearers and to the Eucharist.

A clear discrepancy emerges from the various reports on Christian experience especially between contemporary Church order—or canon law—and a variety of practices to do with office in the Church, especially in what are known as basic communities. In the light of the whole tradition of the Church—one of the spheres of our own theological investigation—how ought we to react to these facts and these reports based on Christian experience? In considering this question, we should bear in mind that, on the one hand, statistics in themselves have no normative value and, on the other, that it is impossible to deny the Christian concern from which these alternative practices emerge.

1. NO CHURCH COMMUNITY WITHOUT A LEADER

Ecclesia non est quae non habet sacerdotes—no Church community without a leader or a team of leaders (with the powers accepted by the Church). When Jerome[1] wrote these words he was obviously expressing the universal view of the early Church. This patristic comment is an anticipatory judgment on the way so many of us take for granted now-adays the shortage of priests in Church communities. If there is, from the sociological point of view, such a shortage of priests, then there must be something wrong with the way in which Christians see their Church and their office-bearers (and with their practice in this respect).

It is not, however, possible to analyse the present shortage of priests—which continues to give rise to secondary phenomena of questionable value with regard to the Church and especially the Eucharist because of its dubious ideological background[2]—purely and simply on sociological and statistical grounds (see J. Kerkhofs' article in this issue). It must also be considered from the historical, theological and ecclesiological points of view. A basically theological examination of the problem is also able to bring to light the obstructions and the previous decisions which are at the origin of this shortage of priests and which ought not to exist from the ecclesiological point of view.

A great deal, but not everything is possible in a Church community. I shall first of all look back very generally at the differently orientated conception of office in the Church during the first ten or so centuries and contrast it with the view that has prevailed during the second Christian millennium. This procedure has not been inspired by an untheological romantic longing to return to the origins of Christianity or by what I believe to be a wrong conviction that chronology—a closeness in time to the New Testament—should as such have priority. In themselves, the first ten centuries of Christianity are in no way to be preferred to the second millennium. What is of fundamental importance here is not chronology, but Christian praxis or *sequala Jesu*. Faithfulness to the New Testament and the great Christian tradition, which is now almost two thousand years old, does not in any way imply repetition—of any period, including that of the New Testament. Our contemporary questions, however, cannot in themselves be normative without a critical recollection of the whole of the Church's past, even though they are a part of that history. A truly Christian answer to these questions can only be obtained, I believe, in a critical confrontation between the present and the past.

I am therefore fundamentally concerned with theological criteria and consequently with the theological significance of the Church's practice with regard to office throughout the centuries in certain changing situations that have been determined by history. The critical point in this connection is whether the Church's practice with regard to office was primarily formed on the basis of theological criteria (although in a definitely historical setting), as was the case during the first ten centuries, or whether it has been fashioned mainly on the basis of extra-theological factors, as has happened in the second millennium.

One of the distinguishing marks of the theologican is his practice of confronting the Church and its living praxis with the whole tradition of faith, all its historically changing contexts and the theological or non-theological models that have, consciously or unconsciously, been invested in that tradition. For all its importance, even the Council of Trent was only one of many regulating factors in the correct interpretation of Scripture, with the result that it does not express the many-sided totality of Christian faith. It only expresses one part of that faith and, what is more, expresses that part in a particular situation that was determined by history. That part is, moreover, exclusive to the Western Church. Even though the Council of Trent expressed 'Christian truth', it was a contextual truth, that is, it was related in a specific way to a definite western situation.

The result of this is that, as far as their significance for us today is concerned, all the statements made by all the Church's councils and, even more importantly, all other non-conciliar pronouncements made by the Church must be interpreted not only within their own historical context, but also within the whole of the Christian tradition of faith, in the context of the orientation and inspiration that this long tradition has given to the further history of the Church in the light of biblical and apostolic faith. Throughout the further development of the Church, this inspiration has been expressed again and again in the best possible way in constantly changing situations. The Christian churches have sometimes succeeded in this. Sometimes they have succeeded less well and at times their achievements have been disappointing. Modern theologians are universally in agreement about this, although the Church's magisterium tends still to attach too much value to the 'letter' of earlier pronouncements and to underestimate their historical and hermeneutical aspects.

We have, therefore, to consider the facts in the early, the mediaeval and the modern history of the Churches if we are to assess the significance of the contemporary and alternative forms of office which are arising everywhere today and which deviate frequently from the valid order in the Church and discover the possible theological value of these ways of exercising office. It is also clear that authoritative documents—the authority of which is accepted by Catholic theologians, although that authority may be changing—have always been produced by a new praxis from below. This happened in the fifth century and characterised the image of the priest during the first millennium. It also took place in the twelfth and thirteenth centuries and fashioned the feudal image of the priest. This new praxis from below in the sixteenth century also resulted in the Tridentine, modern and therefore recent and traditional image of the priest. Official documents have again and again sanctioned the Church's practice that has come about from below.

We are at the present moment witnessing all around us the emergence from below of further new alternative or parallel conceptions and practices with regard to the Church's office. These have a clear affinity to the biblical and the patristic understanding of office. In the fairly distant future, then, after a probable process of purification, we may expect what may be called the contemporary 'fourth' phase in the Church's practice with regard to office to be ultimately sanctioned canonically. Critical recollections of past history therefore have the power to open up the future for us.

A. The First Millennium: A Pneumatological and Ecclesial Conception of Office

I. The Apostolicity of the 'Community of Christ'

On the basis of the New Testament,[3] the early Church was conscious of its apostolicity. What does 'apostolic' mean here? In the first place, it means the Christian communities' consciousness that they are built on the foundation of the 'apostles and prophets' of the earliest Church. According to the New Testament, living community is a community of believers who take over as their own the Jesus thing, that is, the kingdom of God that is to come as a phenomenon that is essentially linked with the whole appearance and ultimately with the person of Jesus and therefore want to preserve the story of and about Jesus in his significance for the future of all men. In this, the emphasis is also, but less on a teaching which has to be kept as pure as possible and more on the 'story' of and about Jesus and on the *sequela Jesu*, that is, a Christian praxis of following Jesus that has to be experienced as radically as possible, according to the orientation and inspiration of the 'kingdom of God and his righteousness' (Matt. 6:33). This is the power of the love of a God who is orientated towards mankind, which is the Christian dream seen as the idea of power making the future: 'Behold, the dwelling of God with men' (Rev. 21:1-4). Basically, what we have here is an assembly of believers, a community in which the vision of 'a new heaven and a new earth' is kept alive with reference to Jesus of Nazareth confessed as 'the Christ, God's only beloved Son, our Lord' and in bearing prophetic witness to conforming to the praxis of this kingdom of God.

This community of God is also a brotherhood in which the power structures dominating the world are broken down (Matt. 20:25-26; Mark 10:42-43; Luke 22:25) and all men are equal, although it might be possible to say that only the least of men, the poor and the oppressed are 'more equal' ('all men are equal, but some are more equal than others'!). All are called, although there are differences in function and, within these functions, even differences of office between the universal commitment of all believers to the community and specifically official ministries, especially that of the leader or the leading team of the community.[4]

Christian churches, then, are, according to the New Testament, apostolic. This includes the apostolic proclamation of Jesus' own message (of the kingdom of God) and Jesus' person, and therefore his death and resurrection cannot be separated from that message: 'The gospel of Jesus Christ, the Son of God' (Mark 1:1) or the 'gospel of God' (Mark 1:14). This apostolicity of the Christian community is placed in a dialectical relationship with the apostolicity of the Church's office (or the so-called *successio apostolica*). The apostolicity of the Christian community after all includes the apostolic mediation of faith and therefore also the lasting importance of thadition.e original document in which the 'gospel of Jesus Christ' is kerygmatically narrated, in other words, the New Testament, which is placed over and against the sphere of understanding of what is known as the Old Testament. The apostolicity of the content of the faith of the community is critical from the point of view of the New Testament: 'What you have heard from me before many witnesses entrust to faithful men who will be able to teach others also' (2 Tim. 2:2). It is primarily less a question of an uninterrupted succession or continuity of office and more a question of an uninterrupted continuity in the apostolic tradition or the content of faith.

It is from this that the fundamental self-understanding of the Christian community is obtained. It is the 'community of Jesus', that is, by gathering as a community around Jesus as salvation in God's name, according to the witness borne by the apostles.

This community has—from the sociological point of view—a right to leaders and, for a community of God, this right is also an apostolic right. As the community of Christ, this community also has, on the basis of Jesus' mandate: 'Do this in memory of me', an ecclesiological right to the celebration of the eucharist. It was, moreover, on the basis of this apostolic orientation that the New Testament communities and the communities of the early Church lived.

From the very beginning there were many offices and ministries in the Church. It cannot be established on the basis of the New Testament that there is only one office that can be historically divided up in descending order into different fragments. (This is a legitimate view, but it is not the only one and it is certainly abstract, unhistorical and purely theological and nothing more than that.) In the constitutive phase of the early Church, the 'apostolate' of those who founded the community—what is known in Scripture as the 'apostles and prophets'—was undoubtedly to some extent unique, but, as soon as the first generation of apostles and prophets had disappeared, the problem of leadership in the Church arose explicitly for all the churches. This problem, which became acute roundabout A.D. 80 to 100, was one which even preoccupied Paul just before his death, which was expected at about that time (see, for example, Phil. 2:19-24). It was also at this time that the Church's office was given concrete, although still very flexible outlines in the different communities and at the same time was subjected to theological reflection as office, even though less interest was taken in the structures of office.

The pace-makers or leaders of the communities had died and the question was: How ought it to go on? On closer inspection, the use of pseudonyms—a fairly universal practice in profane circles in the ancient world—provides us with a positive view of the meaning of this practice. New leaders, who had often previously been collaborators with the apostles or 'spontaneous' leaders, followed in the footsteps of the founders of communities or of those who had maintained the tradition of the Church in certain communities—such men as Paul, Peter, Barnabas, James and a certain John. When these new leaders wrote letters to their communities, these were written in the name of the apostle who had been the tradition-bearer of the community in question. The Pastoral Epistles (Titus and 1 and 2 Timothy) were, for example, written as though they had been written by the Apostle Paul himself (although the latter was by that time already dead). It is precisely because the communities, together with their leaders, thought of themselves as 'Pauline', for example, that the letters written by their new leaders were originally attributed by the communities themselves to Paul. It is clear from this that these communities consciously wished to think of themselves as 'apostolic' communities—as communities of the Jesus who had been proclaimed by the 'apostles and prophets' as the crucified but risen Jesus. An entire theology of the 'apostolic community' and the 'Church's office' is concealed within this pseudonymity.

The transition from the original Church to the post-apostolic churches (which are still New Testament churches) is clear from Eph. 4:7-10 and 4:11-16. After their death, these apostles and prophets, together with other founders of communities were called the foundation of the Church (Eph. 2:20). The new leaders, who were then, in that Church, called 'evangelists, pastors and teachers' (Eph. 4:11; and see 2:20; 3:6), had to continue to build on the foundation that had already been laid. The post-apostolic community leaders were therefore characterised by two inseparable qualifications. On the one hand, they were, like the apostles (1 Cor. 4:1; Rom. 10:14-15, 17), in the name of Christ in his service. On the other, however, the new situation, in contrast to the first Christian generations, was to be found in the fact that the Church office-bearers knew that they were bound to the apostolic inheritance. The post-apostolic office-bearers had therefore to take care of the original apostolic experience from which the communities had to live. They had, in other words, to safeguard Christian identity and evangelical vitality.

In this, office was clearly embedded in the whole complex of other ministries that were needed for the building up of the community (Eph. 4:11). The specific and distinctive character of the charisma of office within many other ministries is to be found in the fact that those bearing office had their own special responsibility, in solidarity with the whole of the community, for maintaining the apostolic identity and the evangelical vitality of the community. What was, from the New Testament point of view, of primary theological importance here was the demand of apostolicity, not the manner of appointment. The apostolicity of the communities founded by the apostles and prophets is, then, the source and the basis of the apostolicity of the Church's office. No historical guarantees can be discovered in any other view.

II. Historical Form within the Church

(a) In A.D. 451, after taking different forms for years in the various Christian communities, but in the long run becoming fairly uniform, this New Testament view was given an official canonical sanction. This is to be found in canon 6 of the Council of Chalcedon. This canon reproduces in a juridical form the view of the New Testament and the early Church of office in the Church. This view is moreover vividly confirmed by patristic theology and various liturgical forms used in the early Church. Not only are all forms of 'absolute ordination' condemned in this canon—they are also declared invalid: 'No one, neither priest nor deacon, may be ordained in an absolute manner (apolelumenos) . . . if he has not been clearly assigned to a local community, either in the city or in the country, either in a martyrium or in a monasterium.' This important text continues: 'The sacred Council concludes that their ordination (cheirotonia) is null and void . . . and that they may not carry out any functions on any occasion.'[5]

What theological view of the Church's office does this statement contain? It is that it is only someone who is called by a definite community to be its leader and pace-maker who may receive ordination. This ordinatio was primarily the accreditation of a believer as office-bearer to a definite community that had itself called this particular fellow-Christian and had designated him as its leader or president or had accepted and confirmed the appearance of one or more of its members in charismatic leadership. An absolute ordination—that is, the designation of someone (cheirotonia) or later laying hands on someone (cheirothesia)—without that candidate having been asked by a particular community to be its leader (or, if he had successfully appeared, without his having been accepted by the community) is, according to this canon of the Council of Chalcedon, null and void.

This canon, then, reveals the fundamentally ecclesial view of office in the early Church. The concept of ordinatio therefore includes not only— and even especially—a bishop's laying on of hands together with epiclesis or prayer to the Holy Spirit, but also—and primarily—being called, appointed or accepted (*cheirotonia*) by a definite Christian community.

The community calls and this is the calling or vocation of the priest, but, because the community regards itself as a 'community of Jesus', the ecclesial appointment is at the same time experienced as a 'gift of the Holy Spirit', in other words, as a pneumatological event. This dialectical bond, formulated canonically, between 'community' and Holy Spirit or between 'community' and 'office' points to the fact that the distinction between the power of ordination and the power of jurisdiction were at that time not only unknown, but also unthinkable from the point of view of ecclesiology.[6] 'No bishop should be imposed on the people if the people do not want him.'[7] 'The one who must lead all the people must be chosen by all the people.'[8]

According to this view, then, office is essentially ecclesial and therefore pneumatologically determined. It depends in no way on a private and ontological qualification of the individual person bearing office and is also in no way separate from an ecclesial context. What is in the balance here is the essential relationship between the community and office. Paulinus of Nola recorded that he was 'ordained' in an absolute manner in Barcelona. He describes this ordination in a tone of pious irony, in words that can be translated as 'There I was, orphaned, dressed in rags and tatters, alone in front of our Lord, a priest without a community' and declares that he was *in sacerdotium tantum Domini, non etiam in locum Ecclesiae dedicatus*.[9] Isidore of Seville called men who had been ordained in an absolute manner men without heads, 'neither a horse nor a man',[10] in other words, neither fish, flesh nor fowl.

The bond between the community and office was so strong in the early Church that is was in principle impossible to be transferred to another community (although there were exceptions to this general principle for reasons of mercy and discretion—the so-called principle of *oikonomia*).[11] Another important consequence of this view of the Church's office was that an office-bearer who, for any reason, ceased to be the leader of a community *ipso facto* became a layman again in the full sense of the word.[12]

The view underlying this concept is this: It is not the possessor of the 'power of ordination' who may lead the community and therefore also lead in the celebration of the eucharist, but the leader who, by being accredited by and to a definite community (that is, *ordinatio* or *cheirotonia*, which is not the same as *cheirothesia* or the laying on of hands), receives all the necessary powers for the leadership of a Christian community. Because the community regarded itself, however, as a 'community of God', the 'Body of the Lord' and the 'temple of the Holy Spirit', a liturgical framework, in which supplication was made for God's charisma to be given to the leader appointed (in other words, *cheirotonia* became *cheirothesia*), was given at a very early date and almost automatically to this accreditation by and to the community. This was, then, not a sacral action, but a *believing sacramentality*.[13]

We may therefore conclude that a situation in which a community was unable to celebrate the Eucharist because there was no bishop or presbyter present was unthinkable in the early Church. As Jerome commented: 'No Church community without a leader'. On the basis of the right of the community to the Eucharist, the leader of the community also has the right to lead in the Eucharist. The community cannot, moreover, live evangelically without the Eucharist because it is a Eucharistic community, that is, a community that celebrates the Eucharist. If there is no leader, it chooses a suitable candidate from its own ranks. What are involved here are the evangelical identity and the Christian identity of the community.

(b) This understanding of office that prevailed in the early Church and was officially recorded in the document of the Council of Chalcedon is also expressed in the earliest known liturgy of the laying on of hands, the *Traditio Apostolica* of Hippolytus, which dates back to the first half of the third century.[14] According to this 'Apostolic Tradition', the whole local community, together with its leaders who were already present in the community, chose its own bishop, its own presbyters and its own deacons.[15] We also know from other texts that the community might expect the one who had been called to accept this mission, even against his own will, because the community had a right to leaders by virtue of its necessary apostolicity, its Christian identity and its evangelical vitality.[16] The local Church put the apostolic faith of the candidate to the test and bore witness to that faith. This is a clear indication of the conviction in the early Church that the community itself is primarily apostolic. Because the leader (who was at that time the bishop) was given a specific responsibility for the apostolic community, it was the community that received the leader which first tested the apostolic foundation of his faith.

Although the local church chose its own leader, it did not give itself its office-bearer in an autonomous way. The choice by a 'community of Christ' was, because of its Christian nature, experienced as a gift of the Holy Spirit. This was expressed liturgically and sacramentally by the laying on of hands by bishops of neighbouring local churches. (From the time of the Council of Nicaea onwards, at least three bishops were required.) In this practice, the communion embracing all Christian churches is vividly expressed, in that it shows that no single local church has a monopoly of the gospel or Christian apostolicity, but is subject to the criticism of the other apostolic churches.

Supplication was made in the prayer or *epiclesis* pronounced over the candidate recommendd by the community as its leader (who was in fact a

H

bishop) for the gift of the 'power of the *pneuma hugemonikon*', the spirit of leadership, and the 'power of the *pneuma archieratikon*', the spirit of high priesthood. Supplication was also made over a member of the episcopal council, the presbyter, for the 'spirit of grace and counsel of the presbyteral college'. Finally, supplication was also made over the deacon, who was at that time completely in the service of the bishop and was able to do anything that he was authorised to by the bishop, having a spiritual charisma 'under the authority of the bishop'.

In this whole procedure, the emphasis is clearly placed, despite certain differences, on the power of the Spirit which proceeds from the Father to the Son and from the Son to the apostles and for which supplication is made by the community which is founded on the apostles together with their leaders over those whom the community has chosen to be its leader (the bishop) and his helpers (the presbyters and deacons). It is interesting to note that Hippolytus has not prescribed any unchangeable formulae in any of the three cases (the episcopate, the presbyterate and the diaconate). As he says himself, his 'Apostolic Tradition' was intended to help leaders to improvise, 'so long as the prayer is soundly orthodox'.[17] No liturgical accreditation or *ordinatio* was required in the case of other ministries in the Church such as those of the catechist, the lector or the sub-deacon.[18]

The pneumatological and ecclesial view of office that prevailed in the early Church also emerges clearly from this liturgy. What comes from below is experienced as coming from the Holy Spirit, with the result that there is no dualism between what comes from below and what comes from above. The important aspect is, moreover, the gift of the power of the Spirit, so that no distinction is made between grace and 'sign'. This is stressed by a section in the 'Apostolic Tradition' on the *confessores-martyres,* that is, those Christians who were arrested because of their faith and who suffered for the Christ thing, but were not, for some chance reason, put to death. Such Christians were believed to possess the charisma of the Spirit because they had borne witness to their faith by suffering. If a community wanted to have such a Christian as its leader (its deacon or presbyter), no laying on of hands was required.[19] By virtue of the power of his faith, he already possessed the necessary power of the Spirit.

It is important, however, to note that even these candidates had to be (liturgically) accredited by and to the community (although the laying on of hands was omitted in their case). This then, is clearly a confirmation of the two aspects of the early idea of *ordinatio*—on the one hand, the ecclesial aspect relating to Church order of an accreditation to the Church and, on the other, the pneumatological and Christological aspect of a charisma of the Spirit. Office in the Church, then, is constituted by being accredited by and to the Church as one bearing office and by being graced with the charisma of the Spirit (whether this takes place institutionally or charismatically). This charisma of the Spirit is different according to the tasks allotted to the candidate by the community.

With regard to the New Testament, the difference in the later Church can be found in the fact that the signs that were originally differentiated in the New Testament were, at the later period, combined in the one episcopate, with the result that the theory emerged that there was only one office—the episcopate—and that all the other offices were only partial tasks, participating in the one episcopate. In my opinion, this is a possible theology which is legitimate, but not necessary. Nonetheless, it is also clear that 'office' in the Church has, from the very beginning, always included collegiality. There has, in other words, always been a united pluralism of Christians provided with different charisms of office.

III. The First 'Sacerdotalisation' of the Church's Office

It is clear from the pre-Nicene literature especially that the early Church found it difficult to call its leaders 'priestly'. According to the New Testament, only Christ and the Christian community were priestly. The leaders were in the service of Christ and the priestly people of God, but they were never called priestly themselves. Cyprian was one of the first Christians to show a clear preference for the Old Testament terminology of the sacrificial priesthood and compared this with the Christian Eucharist.

In this way, there was a gradual sacerdotalisation of the vocabulary of the Church's office,[20] although this was initially used in the allegorical sense. Cyprian was also the first to say that the *sacerdos*, that is, the bishop as the leader of the community and therefore also in the Eucharist, acted in this capacity *vice Christi*, that is, in the place of Jesus.[21] Augustine, on the other hand, refused to call bishops and presbyters 'priests' in the sense of mediators between Christ and the community.[22]

With his 'Apostolic Tradition', Hippolytus is obviously at a transitory stage. In his *epiclesis*, he speaks simply of the 'Spirit of the high priesthood' that is attributed to the episcopal leader. On the other hand, however, he says again and again that the bishop is *as* a high priest (*Traditio Apostolica* 3 and 34), which points to continuing influence of the Old Testament and the patristic use of allegory. These comparisons are, however, not made in connection with the presbyters, who are therefore clearly seen as non-priestly, although they were (to varying degrees according to the different local communities) increasingly permitted, as time passed, to replace the bishop in leading in the Eucharist (without needing a new 'ordination' to do this).

It is therefore hardly possible to speak of priests in connection with both bishops and presbyters in the pre-Nicene period of the Church's history. In the early Church, the Old Testament name for Jewish priests—*sacerdos*—was used in an allegorical sense and even then it was initially only employed in connection with the bishop,[23] who was at that time the figure in whom the local community identified itself and found its unity. In the long run, however, presbyters also normally came to lead in the celebration of the Eucharist (because they were in fact the local leaders of smaller communities) and for this reason they too came ultimately to be called *sacerdotes* or 'priests'. They were, however, still known as priests *secundi meriti*, in other words, priests who were subordinate to the episcopal leader.[24] This, then, was the beginning of the process of sacerdotalisation at least of the vocabulary used in connection with those holding office in the Church.

IV. Priestly Office-Bearers and the Eucharist

There would at first sight seem to be a connection between the 'priesthood' and the Eucharist in the light of the development outlined in the preceding section. This is, however, not the case, at least as far as the whole truth is concerned. In the early Church there was an essential connection between the community and leader of the community and therefore also between the leader of the community and the the community that celebrates the Eucharist. This is an essential nuance in this context.

It is a fact that the 'Church's office' did not develop in the New Testament from and around the Eucharist. It did, however, develop from and around the apostolicity of the community, that is, from the need to proclaim and admonish and to build up and lead the community. In whatever way the word is used, 'office' has to to with leading the community. It was apparently not a separate problem for the New Testament authors as to who had to lead in the Eucharist, since none of them tell us anything about it. Paul does not call the Eucharist an apostolic tradition, but a tradition from the Lord himself (see 1 Cor. 11:23), to which even the apostles were bound.

The Eucharist was, after all, Jesus' parting gift to the whole of his community: 'Do this in memory of me'. As the community of Christ, then, the community has an inalienable right to the celebration of the Eucharist. There is no indication anywhere in the New Testament of an explicit link between the Church's office and presiding at the Eucharist. This does not, however, mean that any believer can lead in the celebration. In the house communities at Corinth, it was the hosts who led in the house celebrations of the Eucharist, but these men were also the leaders of the same house communities. In any case, what can be said with certainty is that a sacral and mystical foundation of the function of the office-bearer in the Eucharist cannot be found anywhere in the New Testament.

This, however, does not mean that the Eucharist is in any way seen in the New Testament as being totally dissociated from the concept of office.[25] There is in fact only one place in which a factual connection is established between 'leaders' and leading in the liturgy and this is a fairly vague reference (Acts 13:1-2). If it is borne in mind that the early Eucharist was modelled on the Jewish table prayer or *bir^ekath hammazôn*, the 'blessing of the food', in which it was certainly not possible for anyone to lead,[26] it should be obvious that the leaders of the community also led in the celebration of the Eucharist by virtue of the fact that they were leaders. This is also clear from texts that appeared at about the same time as the last part of the New Testament. 'Prophets and teachers' were the leaders in the Eucharist according to the earliest level of the Didache and 'presbyters' according to the later level. All of these, moreover, led in an official capacity.[27] In the First Epistle of Clement, the bishop-presbyters led.

We may therefore summarise the general view in this way. Whoever was competent to lead the community was also *ipso facto* the leader in the Eucharist. (In this sense, leading in the Eucharist does not need to be a separate competence or power, apart from being the competence of the leader of the community.) What we have here is clearly the 'presidency of the community' (essentially exercised by an individual or in a team): 'We receive the sacrament of the Eucharist . . . from no one other than the president of the community'.[28]

This aspect was stressed in the Church from the time of Ignatius of Antioch onwards. At that time, the bishop was in fact the leader of the community and for this reason no Eucharist was to be celebrated in opposition to the bishop's will.[29] Both in the case of Ignatius and in that of Cyprian later, the underlying intention here was to preserve the unity of the community. The figure of unity in the community therefore also led in the Eucharist, which Cyprian described as the 'sacrament of Church unity'.[30] Although the problem of office also played a part here, what was primarily at stake was the apostolicity and the unity of the Church: 'No Eucharist outside the community of the Church'.[31] What is stressed in this teaching is above all that a 'heretical' community has no right to the Eucharist. Even in the case of Ignatius, the question of the official leader in the Eucharist is subordinate.

What is more, in the early Church the whole of the believing community concelebrated under the leadership of the leader of the community. According to a later, but still early *Liber Pontificalis*, everyone concelebrated (*tota aetas concelebrat*).[33] Some scholars have inevitably asked whether *concelebrare* had exactly the same meaning then as it had now. Was it used in the early Church in the same technical sense as it has been used in the second Christian millennium? The critical counter-question that seems most appropriate is: On what grounds can we give theological priority to a narrower technical meaning? This may, after all, equally well be a narrowing of vision. Leading in the Eucharist in the early Church was only the liturgical aspect of a much more diverse official presidency in the Christian community. The one who was recognised as the pace-maker in the community also led in the Eucharist.

In the early Church, moreover, the community itself was the active subject of the *offerimus panem et calicem*.[34] The specific function of the *sacerdos* who leads in the Eucharist should not be defined in the light of later interpolations into liturgical books. (Examples of this practice are: *Accipe potestatem offerre sacrificium* and *sacerdos oportet offerre*. Such interpolations assume a later *potestas sacra* in the priest that is isolated from the community and therefore absolute.)

In the solemn Eucharist (which was initially improvised), that is, the thanks and praise or anaphora spoken by the leader, the latter appeared primarily as the prophetic leader of the community with pastoral respon-sibility for that community who proclaimed the history of salvation and therefore praised and thanked God and in this way announced the presence of salvation to the assembled community. It was for this reason that the leader took the gifts offered by the whole community which were transformed by the Holy Spirit into the gift of Jesus' body and blood.

It has been pointed out by many theologians, including, for example, Y. Congar, D. Droste, R. Schultze, K. J. Becker and R. Berger, that the integral subject of all liturgical action—and this includes the action of the Eucharist—in the early Church was the *ecclesia* itself, never the 'I' of the leader alone.[35] Concelebration was therefore not limited at that time to a shared celebration of the Eucharist by concelebrating priests. It was an action performed by the whole believing people present.[36] The people celebrated and the priest only led in service. Even when it is clear that concelebrating priests are meant, there was only one leader and the others concelebrated silently. The *recitatio communis* (regarded as neces-sary for 'concelebration') is not mentioned in the early Church.[37] This is why the Eucharist could always take place in the early Church in the assembly of the community.

V. Laymen as Leaders?

The question as to whether a lay person may lead in the Eucharist is a modern question. For the early Church, it was a wrong way of posing the problem. In the first place, it was the bishop who, albeit in collegial association with his presbyters, was the leader of the community and it was therefore he who also led in the Eucharist and who was alone in this.

He was, as we have seen, the ecclesial figure of unity. Gradually (with the growth of the communities, which were originally cities, into what we would now call 'provinces' of the Church) his non-priestly helpers or presbyters obtained permission to lead in the Eucharist in his absence (although they had not in any sense been ordained to do this). The point of departure in the discussion of this question in the First Epistle of Clement is that the episcopos-presbyter normally led in the Eucharist. The author, however, adds: 'or other eminent persons . . . with the full consent of the whole Church', since 'everything must take place in accordance with order'.[38]

The acceptance of a leader by the Church was therefore clearly of decisive importance. Ignatius, who called the bishop, as the figure by whom the community identified itself, the real leader in the Eucharist, at the same time also recognised cases in which it was possible and permissible for him to be replaced.[39] He does not mention presbyters or deacons explicitly as potential replacements in this context.

We do, however, have one, and only one explicit testimony in the early Church to the fact that, in emergencies, a layman was permitted to lead in the Eucharist. Tertullian, who nonetheless makes a clear distinction between *ordo* (official accreditation to and by the community) and *plebs*, the believing people or 'laity', says that it was by definition the leader of the community who led in normal circumstances in the Eucharist and, for Tertullian, this meant the bishop together with his council of presbyters. All the same, he also notes: 'Where there is no college of accredited servants, you, layman, must lead in the Eucharist and baptise. Then you are your own priest, for, where two or three are gathered together, there is the Church, even if all those are lay people'.[40]

In exceptional circumstances, the community therefore chose its own leader *ad hoc*.[41] Although Augustine was opposed to the sacerdotalisation of the Church's office-bearers, a process making the bishop or presbyter a mediator between God and the people, he explicitly denies that the layman had any right to lead in the Eucharist, even in emergencies.[42] Tertullian did not make his statement under the influence of Montanism. On the contrary, he criticises the Montanists for letting laymen lead in the Eucharist although there was no extreme emergency and in this way denied the specific character of the Church's office.[43]

In holding this view, Tertullian was not so isolated in the early Church as it might at first sight seem, even though the unstable terminology clearly played a part in this question. Anyone who was invited in such circumstances by the community to lead in the community (and therefore also in the Eucharist) was, by the very fact that he was accepted by the Church (the early practice of *cheirotonia*), *ipso facto* an office-bearer. He was 'accredited', in other words, he had power and competence as the leader of the community. It was this that Augustine had in mind, with the result that there was, despite the differences in terminology, a real consensus. The specific character of the Church's office was defended by everyone. What was not defended was a power of sacral ordination or a concrete manner of official accreditation.

We must now consider the view with regard to the Church's office that came to prevail in the second millennium. In contrast to those that we have just discussed, the new and later conception expressed an exclusive concentration on office as such and a greatly reduced emphasis on *ecclesia*. It was also above all a juridical view in which the concepts of sacrament and law were dissociated from each other.

B. The Second Millennium: A Direct Christological Foundation and a Privatisation of Office

Two Latin councils of the Church, the Third Lateran Council (1179) and the Fourth Lateran Council (1215) sanctioned, in principle, a fairly radical re-interpretation of the early Church view of office. Gratian had mentioned canon 6 of the Council of Chalcedon, which forbade all absolute ordinations and declared them to be invalid, in his twelfth century *Decretum*, and even before this, towards the end of the eleventh century, the theologian Hugh of Saint Victor had referred to this same canon.[44] The fact remains, however, that both the Third and the Fourth Lateran Council broke away from the view expressed at Chalcedon, not only in principle, but also in fact.

It was, then, the *titulus Ecclesiae* on which a man could, according to the Council of Chalcedon, be ordained (in other words, a man could only be 'ordained' if he had been recommended or accepted as leader by a definite community) that was quite fundamentally re-interpreted in 1179, during the pontificate of Alexander III. According to the new interpretation of this early ecclesiological *titulus Ecclesiae*, no one could be ordained 'if a reasonable livelihood had not been assured'.[45] This was not, at least in principle, a denial of the early ecclesial practice of accreditation to and by the community, but it was a new way of looking at that accreditation—in view of the difficulties encountered in feudal society, accreditation was seen in the light of the priest's ability to support himself or be supported financially.

I conclude that there was no intention of breaking radically with the past at the Third Lateran Council because, 20 years after that Council, Pope Innocent III once again—and for the last time in the history of the Church!—recalled, in 1198, the invalidity of absolute ordinations. (He also added that, on grounds of mercy and in accordance with an old practice of *oikonomia*, priests who had been ordained in an absolute manner might be allowed to continue to exercise their functions on condition that their bishops provided for their upkeep. This is evidence of a compromise between patristic and feudal views.)

In view of the prevailing economic conditions and the number of members of the clergy who led a wandering life (as well as the existence of many 'private' churches founded by worldly lords), the provision of financial support for the clergy was an urgent and painful question at that time. This does not, however, mean that the early *titulus Ecclesiae* was not reduced to a purely feudal matter of a benefice. This change took place on the surface and the early Christian undercurrent was not denied. It was, however, the changed surface that was accepted into the new scholastic theology, with the result that only it was recognised centuries later at the Council of Trent, which sanctioned it in the twenty-third session (1563).[46] To summarise, then, a man has or feels that he has a vocation to the priesthood. He makes an application (this shows that the ecclesial bond had not been completely lost) and is trained for the priesthood and finally ordained. Everything is settled and he only has to wait to know where his bishop will send him. *Ordinatio* continues to be an accreditation of the priest as an office-bearer to a diocesan region, it is true, but the concrete place or community to which he will be sent remains open. What has completely disappeared in this procedure is the call of the community, which was in the early Church the essential element of ordination.

The Third Lateran Council undoubtedly made a clear dividing line between the first and the second Christian millennia in this respect and this change was emphasised by the pronouncement made by the Fourth Lateran Council that the Eucharist could only be celebrated by a 'validly ordained priest'.[47] In itself, of course, this statement is not necessarily in contradiction with the conviction that prevailed in the first Christian millennium, but it is certainly a narrowing down of that conviction. The essential bond that had existed for centuries with the choice made by the community is absent and the ecclesial aspect of the Eucharist is reduced to the 'celebrating priest'.

The full extent of this narrowing down of the vision of the Church's office is clear both from what preceded and from what followed these two councils. It is evident that this fairly radical change did not take place on the basis of theological criteria, but above all for non-theological reasons. It is also certain that the effects of these two councils in this respect at least were not the result of theological intuitions, but rather the consequence of non-theological presuppositions. It is only this which justifies the theological priority of the earlier ecclesial view of the Church's office over the view which is now regarded as valid.

It is certainly possible to ask how this fundamental change in the

Church's view of its own office-bearers was able to come about in history. We cannot, of course, analyse the whole phenomenon of feudal society, which is clearly essentially important in this question. Certain historians have blamed the emergence, precisely at the time of the Third and Fourth Lateran Councils, of the theory of a mysterious sacramental character, which formed the basis of the whole theology of the *sacramentum ordinis*.[48] I believe that these scholars are wrong, especially since this very vague theory of the character, dating back to the end of the twelfth century, was nonetheless interpreted in all its medieval modernity by all the leading scholastic theologians—Bonaventure, Albert the Great and especially Thomas Aquinas—in continuity with the early Church.

For these theologians, whose interpretations show certain divergencies, this character points to the visible bond between *ecclesia* and *ministerium*.[49] (A character, was, moreover, associated with all ordinations and consecrations, from that of the bishop to that of the acolyte or the sacristan, a factor that can only be explained ontologically with some difficulty.) The word *mancipatio*, in other words, being called and accepted by a Christian community for a definite service or ministry in the Church, was the most sensitive aspect of the character in the Middle Ages and this is essentially in keeping with the view of office in the early Church.

The first official document that refers to a priestly character is a letter from Gregory IX in 1231 to the Archbishop of Paris.[50] The scholastic theologians had, from the beginning of the thirteenth century onwards, stressed the bond between the community of the Church and the sacrament of ordination in their teaching about the character, thus following the conviction that prevailed in the early Church, despite the new armoury of concepts that they used. Seen from the dogmatic point of view, however, the only formulation was that of the existence of the character. What is more, the Council of Trent clearly wanted to leave the field free for further theological explanations, including the view held by certain theologians that the character was only a *relatio rationis*, that is, a logical relationship and a juridical fiction. (This was the opinion of Durandus of Saint-Pourçain among others.)

It is clear, then, that it is not possible to base the ontological view of the priestly character on conciliar pronouncements.[51] This character is a medieval category in which the early Church view of the lasting relationship between the community and the office-bearer on the one hand and between the office-bearer and the gift of the charisma of the Spirit are expressed. In the middle ages, a distinction was made in this charisma of office between the power entrusted in this office (expressed in terms of a *sacra potestas*) and the 'sacramental grace' that is appropriate to that power. This grace was personal to the one bearing office and enabled him, it was argued, to exercise that official power in a holy and Christian way. It can be said that the process of ontological sacerdotalisation was furthered by this distinction made in the charisma of office,[52] but no more than this was achieved by it.

The scholastic doctrine of the character contained certain factors which gave rise, through the medium of other developments, to an ontological and sometimes even magical sacerdotalisation of the priesthood. I would like to point to two main factors that furthered this development. In whatever way the character was interpreted in the Middle Ages, ontologically or juridically or even as a juridical fiction, it was in general seen as a direct participation in the high priesthood of Christ. As Thomas Aquinas declared, along with other medieval theologians of 'modern' outlook: 'The sacramental character is a certain participation in the priesthood of Christ'.[53] This conviction does not in itself need to include an ontologisation of the Church's office (especially in view of the divergent interpretations of the character), but it does lead to an obscuring of the Church's mediation and to an emphasis on the priest as a mediator between Christ and men, a view that Augustine regarded as heretical.

The main reason for the change that took place in the Middle Ages in the Christian view of office is, I believe, to be found in the revival of interest in Roman law towards the end of the eleventh and at the beginning of the twelfth centuries. It is not, in my opinion, to be found in the sacramental character as such (as many historians wrongly believe).[54] Because of this revival of interest, the power of leadership (in every sphere of life) was juridically dissociated from the concept of territoriality. In the sphere of Church life, this means a dissociation from the concept of the local church. (In this context, territoriality and the local church community should not be seen in the purely geographical sense, but understood as 'human space'.) This situation led at the end of the thirteenth century to the well known statement made by Vincent of Beauvais: *Quodque principi placuit, legis habet vigorem*.[55] The principle in this case is that of the *plenitudo potestatis*, in other words, authority as a value in itself, isolated from the community, both in the secular sphere and in the Church. (This was also connected with the struggle about investiture between the *sacerdotium* and the *imperium*.)

It was, then, non-theological, feudal and juridical factors that made the 'medieval' theological change with regard to the Church's office possible. What is more, the dividing line between the 'Spirit of Christ' and the 'spirit of the world' for the Christian was previously to be found in his baptism, his conviction that he had been accepted into the chosen community of God's *ecclesia*, although (as the Church expanded) this dividing line was to some extent shifted to the 'second' baptism, that of the Christian's monastic profession.

Monks had previously been laymen, not priests. For the Christian community, these religious represented their own ideal. The dividing line was, however, shifted even further by the Carolingian Council of Aachen and especially as a result of the Gregorian reforms. At a time when 'everyone' was baptised, the dividing line between the 'Spirit of Christ' and the 'spirit of the world' was placed close to the clergy, who were then the representatives of the Church *par excellence*. The priesthood came to be seen as a personal status in life rather than as an official ministry in the community. It was, in other words, personalised and privatised.[56] What is more, the new ideas about law (*ius*) and jurisdiction led to a division between the *potestas iurisdictionis* and the *potestas ordinis* and a consequent watering down of the earlier concept of 'sacramental right' (a right based on the *sacramentum*).

This is, in my opinion, the fundamental reason why the second Christian millennium became so different from the first. This difference opened the door to absolute ordinations, in which the earlier concept of *ordinatio* became a sacral ordination. This type of ordination made it possible for all kinds of new ideas and practices, which would have been ecclesiologically unthinkable in the first millennium, to arise—practices such as the private mass.[57] A man could be in himself a priest. Many of these new practices were simply not possible in the early Church.

The most important consequence of all these changes is that the earlier relationship between *ecclesia* and *ministerium*, that is, between the community and the Church's office, was transformed into a relationship between *potestas* and *eucharistia*. (This change was made easier by a parallel alteration in the term *corpus verum Christi*. In the early Church, this term referred to the community of the Church. Later, it became the *corpus mysticum Christi* or Eucharistic body. In the Middle Ages, the meaning was quite the reverse.)[58] In the Middle Ages, the priest, who had previously led in the community and had, in other words, been 'accredited' to and by the community in order to lead it, was 'ordained' in order to be able to celebrate the Eucharist.[59] The medieval view of the *sacra potestas* had played a part in this and ordination came to be seen as the conferring of a special power in order that the person given that power might celebrate the Eucharist. The Fourth Lateran Council reacted with logical consistency to this development and declared that only a validly ordained priest was able to pronounce the words of consecration validly.[60] This, however, a juridical narrowing down of the original intention in the early Church.

C. The Modern Image of the Priest

During the period of the *ancien régime* in particular, when men were preoccupied with the idea of absolute monarchy, the changed theological view of leadership in the Church that had at least partly been conditioned by the feudal structure of society and the renewed interest in Roman law resulted in an image of the priest that was clearly formulated for the first time by Josse Clichtove (1472-1543). This image of the priest had a deep influence on the Tridentine teaching about the priesthood and on the whole of priestly spirituality during the sixteenth and seventeenth centuries. It was also further elaborated by Pierre de Bérulle and the French school and formed the background to all the spiritual writing about the priesthood in recent centuries up to the time of the Second Vatican Council.[61]

Biblical, patristic and scholastic ideas were connected in this modern image of the priest with the new situation brought about in modern society. The priest was seen, in a hierarchically structured Christian society governed by a power based on divine law, as a man set apart from the world and lay people (who were responsible for the 'secular' reality). Clichtove saw the Christian priesthood as an extension of the levitical priesthood in a theocratic society.

The basis of this modern spirituality of the priesthood is the sacramental grace of the priest. The priesthood came to be seen as sacrificial and to be experienced in society in the priestly state, which gradually assumed more and more monastic characteristics. Priestly celibacy was no longer seen (as it had been, for example, by Thomas Aquinas) as a purely disciplinary measure in the Church,[62] but was almost attributed to divine law and, as far as its spirituality was concerned, was regarded as forming an essential part of the state of the priesthood as set apart from that of the laity.

The modern image of the priest, then, is completely clerical and hierarchical. Luther and Erasmus had fulminated against the decline of priestly morals and, in reaction against this decline, the Catholic reformer or priestly spirituality, Josse Clichtove, correctly defended the spirituality, of the priest, but he did this by pouring it into a juridical mould. The priesthood thus came, in his teaching, to be placed in the light of an absolute value given to law. Only part of the foundation for this development had been laid in the Middle Ages with its image of the priest. What we have had in the second Christian millennium, then, from the sixteenth century onwards especially, has been a distinctively modern and juridical tightening up of the medieval image of the priest. In the twentieth century, an important contribution has been made by Pius X, Pius XI and Pius XII, making this modern image of the priest more popular.[63]

Despite a certain continuity, it is possible, then, to distinguish three images of the priest (which are also socially conditioned) in the history of the Church. These are the patristic, the medieval and the modern images of the priest. On the basis of a renewed sensitivity to man, society and the Church, contemporary critics of the priesthood are above all preoccupied with the modern image of the priest.

2. CONTINUITY AND DIVERGENCE BETWEEN THE FIRST AND THE SECOND MILLENNIA

A. *The Pneuma-Christological Basis of Office in the Early Church and the Non-Ecclesial Christological Basis of Office in the Modern Church*

Despite the peculiarly Latin and Western aspect of the theology of office that has developed in the Roman Catholic Church since the twelfth century, there are two underground lines of continuity running through the entire two thousand years of tradition in the Christian experience of office in the Church. On the one hand, there is the continuous opposition, which can be clearly distinguished in the early, the medieval and the modern Church, to the celebration of the Eucharist in which the idea of the universal *communio ecclesialis* is rejected or denied. On the other hand, there is both the early and the modern conviction that no Christian community can ultimately and autonomously itself be the final source of its own office-bearers.

In the first Christian millennium and during the pre-Nicene period especially, Christians expressed their view of office above all in an ecclesial and pneumatological way, in other words, in terms of what might be called a Pneuma-Christology. During the second millennium, however, the Church's office has been given a directly Christological basis and both the ecclesial mediation and the part played by the Holy Spirit have been thrust into the background. What has arisen in the second millennium has been a theology of office without an ecclesiology. This movement began in the Middle Ages, when a Christology that lacked a fully elaborated independent ecclesiology that mediated that Christology was followed by the so-called treatise on the sacraments. Although Thomas, for example, always spoke of *sacramenta Ecclesiae*, the sacrament was later defined, in a technically abstract way, as a *signum efficax gratiae*, in which the ecclesial aspect was suppressed and the sacramental power was directly based on the *sacra potestas* that the priest personally possessed. In the way, the ecclesial and charismatic significance of office and its pneumatological meaning became obscured and it became at the same time increasingly enclosed within a juridical framework and dissociated from the sacrament of the Church.

Although in many respects Vatican II returned to the theological insights of the early Church, the view of the Council regarding office in the Church and especially the terminology employed in the relevant conciliar documents express an unmistakable compromise between these two great blocs of tradition in the Church.[64] The ecclesial aspect of office is once again stressed in *Lumen Gentium* and words such as *ministeria* and *munera* are used in preference to *potestas*. The term *potestas sacra* occurs several times, but the classical terms—*potestas ordinis* and *potestas iurisdictionis*—cannot be found anywhere in the document. There is, on the contrary, a clear break with these two parallel terms, in the sense that the power of jurisdiction is essentially already given with ordination. At least fundamentally, then, the early view of the *titulus Ecclesiae* of office has been restored to a place of honour and, at least a beginning has been made to breaking the juridical stranglehold on the Church's office.

B. *'Priest' and 'Lay'*

Quite soon after the New Testament period, following the Jewish model, in which a distinction was made between high priests and the people,[65] a similar distinction was also made, for example, in the First Epistle of Clement, between *klerikos* and *laikos*.[66] These two terms do not, however, point to a distinction of status between 'priest' and 'lay'. A man was *klerikos* if he occupied an office or *kleros*.[67] What we have here is a functional distinction, not in official functions, but in charismatic functions of a specific kind within the Church.[68]

In the light of the whole tradition of the Church, the distinction between priest and lay must be interpreted as an affirmation of a specifically and sacramentally ecclesial function, not as a separate status in the Church. Even in the Middle Ages, theologians refused to regard the relationship between priests and lay people as a relationship between *praelatio* and *subiectio*.[69] The Church is a brotherhood and the dilemma between an ontological and sacerdotalistic view of office on the one hand and a purely functionalistic view on the other must therefore be overcome in and through the theological concept of office in the Church as the gift of the Spirit of an ecclesial charisma of office and as the ministry of leadership in the community and everything that this implies in a community of Christ.

C. *Sacramental Office*

It is clear from this that there has always been a non-sacral, but nonetheless sacramental meaning of office which was therefore correctly associated, even in the early Church, with a liturgical accreditation.[70] From the ecumenical point of view, the question of the technical meaning of the word 'sacrament' must at present remain open, but we are bound to recognise that, from the point of view of content, all the Christian churches that acknowledge the principle and practice of office are agreed about the essential elements constituting what the early Church called *ordinatio*. These are, as we have already said, the candidate's being called or accepted by the community (this is the ecclesial aspect) and the charisma of the Spirit (the Pneuma-Christological aspect). In normal circumstance, these elements are, as we have seen, linked by an official laying on of hands accompanied by an *epiclesis*. In this way, both the ecclesial and the pneumatic aspects of office are given concrete liturgical form in the shared celebration of the community.[71] The Greek Orthodox theologian J. D. Zizioulas has expressed the increasing consensus of opinion among theologians of different confessions. We may summarise what he has said in the following way:[72] The sacramental office is the act through which the community realises itself. Without provoking any contrast between 'charisma' on the one hand and 'office' (or 'accreditation') on the other, the charisma of office is essentially an accreditation or *ordinatio* which is ecclesial by being related to the community, pneumatological and sacramentally juridical. The so-called validity or ecclesial character of ordination is not strictly speaking connected to an isolated sacramental action on the part of the Church (although it normally is in practice and, what is more, connected to the liturgical action of laying on of hands). It is rather connected to the action of the Church community as a whole, that is, as an apostolic community in communion with all other local churches. From the point of view of the Bible and the teaching of the early Church, we are therefore, in the light of this view, justified in giving a positive ecclesiological evaluation to the extraordinary ministry of office, that is, a minitry carried out in exceptional circumstances.

D. *The Christian Community is a Community that Celebrates the Eucharist*

For both the early Church and the modern Church (especially since the Second Vatican Council), it is not possible to think of a Christian community without the celebration of the Eucharist. There is an essential connection between the local *ecclesia* and the Eucharist. Following the Jewish model, at least 12 fathers of families (and therefore 12 families) gathered together in the pre-Nicene Church had a right to a leader and therefore to someone who would lead the community in the celebration of the Eucharist.[73] In the case of smaller communities outside the cities, the original leader (who was a bishop) was soon replaced by a presbyter or 'pastor'.

What we may in any case conclude from this is that the early Church regarded a shortage of priests as impossible, even though, of course, the problem was never expressed in this way. The contemporary shortage of priests can therefore be subjected to the criticism of the view of office held in the early Church, because this modern shortage has origins that lie outside the sphere of the Church's office itself. At present there are clearly more than a sufficient number of Christians, both men and women, who possess this charisma in the ecclesiological sense. These include, for example, the many catechists working in Africa and the many pastoral workers of both sexes in Europe and elsewhere. These Christians do in fact lead in their communities and are pace-makers and figures by whom the communities can identify themselves. They are, however, at the same time prevented in fact from being 'accredited' liturgically for reasons that are extrinsic to the essential character of the Church's office. They cannot therefore lead in the Eucharist and the service of reconciliation. From the ecclesiological point of view, this is a very wrong situation.

E. *Office and the Universal Church*

We must finally consider the relationship between office in a local church and office in the universal Church. In the ancient world, the universal Church was not regarded as a reality that was superior to the local churches. In the beginning, there was no supraregional organisation, although patriarchates and metropolitan churches soon developed and local churches were included within them in a unity that went beyond the city framework. During the first five centuries, the 'primacy of the union of love' of the patriarchal *Sedes Romana* or the Chair of Peter in Rome became increasingly recognised.[74]

The early idea of the universal Church was taken up again by the Second Vatican Council. According to the conciliar Constitution on the Church, it was 'in and from such individual churches' that 'there comes into being the one and only Catholic Church'.[75] The universal Church is made present in the local church and the Christian belongs to the universal Church because he belongs to a local church, not vice versa. It is precisely for this reason that no single church is able to have a monopoly of God's Spirit. It is also possible for Christian communities to criticise each other in the spirit of the gospel. Christian solidarity with other Christian communities is also an essential aspect of even the smallest basic communities in the Church. This kind of ecclesial concern cannot be referred to higher authorities.

This is also the reason why the presence of spokesmen and leaders from neighbouring local communities has always, since the earliest Christian times, been required at the liturgical accreditation of particular Christians as office-bearers to and by a particular community. Within this structure, local office-bearers also have the task of governing the universal Church, the union of love, as critical spokesmen and leaders of their own communities. According to the Catholic view, they are also in solidarity with

I

that leader of the local community who, as the ultimately binding factor, has the Petrine function in the Church.

3. A CRITICAL THEOLOGICAL EVALUATION OF CONTEMPORARY ALTERNATIVE FORMS OF OFFICE

It should be clear from this historical and theological outline that the constant factor in the Church's office can be found only in concrete and historically changing forms. My point of departure in this evaluation is an insight that all Christians may be assumed to share, namely that Church order, however much it may change, is a very great good for Christian communities. In one form or another, Church order forms part of the concrete and essential appearance of the 'communities of God', the Church. This Church order, however, is not there simply for its own sake. Like the Church's office, it is also at the service of the apostolic communities. It cannot be an aim in itself, nor can it be given an absolute value. This is all the more important because it is clear that Church order has at all times in the Church been firmly rooted in history. Certain forms of Church order that have been brought about by particular situations in the Church and society in the past (and therefore certain criteria for the admission of office-bearers in the Church as well) reach, at a certain moment in time, their ultimate limits—there is clear sociological evidence of this in man's concrete experience of the shortcomings of Church order of a particular kind in changed circumstances.

Changes in the dominant image of man and the world, social and economic upheavals and new socio-cultural attitudes and emotions can all lead to a situation in which the Church order that has developed in history contradicts or even prevents what it sought to safeguard in the past, namely the building up of a Christian community. From such an experience of contrast, experiments in new possibilities of Christian and Church life can spontaneously arise (as indeed they did in New Testament times). Experiences of what is defective in any given system have a regulatory value. It is, of course, obvious that even a fairly unanimous experience of what has in fact gone wrong in a valid Church order that has developed in the course of history does not in any sense imply that there will necessarily be complete agreement about how that order should be put right. That can only emerge from the experience of putting a number of new models to the test. These may fail—they are, after all, experiments. Failure is in no way reprehensible—it is simply one phase in the search for a new Christian discovery. What is gradually revealed in all these attempts is the obligatory character of the new possibilities of life for the Church that are required but have not yet been given a concrete form.

It is also an indisputable sociological fact that, in changed times, there is always a danger of ideological fixation with regard to the existing Church order because there is always a great deal of inertia in the case of an established system which is frequently orientated towards self-preservation. This applies, of course, to every system in human society, but it is particularly true of the institutional Church which rightly regards itself as the community of God, but often wrongly displays a tendency to identify old, even venerable traditions with unchangeable divine dispensations. Even the Second Vatican Council displays much more caution in this respect than many of us believed to be the case at the time of the Council itself. One example of this in our present context is that there is a suggestion in the Tridentine document on the 'sacrament of order' that the threefold division in 'holy orders'—the episcopate, the presbyterate and the diaconate—goes back to divine law.[77] The Second Vatican Council replaced this *divina ordinatione* ('by divine dispensation') of the Tridentine canon by the words 'from antiquity'.[78]

Against the background of the existing Church order, then, new and sometimes urgently required alternative possibilities are often only to be seen through the medium of what is bound to be regarded as at least temporarily illegal. This is not a new phenomenon in the Church—it has always been the case. In the early and high Middle Ages, when scholasticism was still very free (in contrast to later scholasticism, which had nothing to say about this fact), this temporary illegality was even raised to the status of a theological principle in the theory of the *non acceptatio legis* or the rejection of the law from above by opposition at the base. Whatever the value of the law may be, it is rejected in certain cases by the majority and thus becomes in fact irrelevant. It is clear from this that there is, in the history of the Church, a way along which Christians can, working from below or from the base, develop a praxis in the Church that may be temporarily in competition with the praxis that is officially valid in the Church at that particular time. This new praxis from below may, however, in its Christian opposition, ultimately even become the dominant praxis of the whole Church and in the long run be sanctioned by the official Church. (And, as history never ceases, the whole process may then begin all over again.)

The various accounts in this issue of *Concilium* of praxis deviating from the official Church order have, I believe, in the first place a threefold effect—of diagnosis, criticism of the existing ideology and dynamism—and, in the second place, a normative value. This normative value is not based on its purely factual nature. It functions as a justified Christian reflection in which a Utopian orientation towards the future is anticipated on the one hand and, on the other, a Christian apostolic conviction that has been tested against the whole history of Christian experience is expressed.

This normative power of factual experience reigns supreme in modern secular society, but none of us would be bold enough to assert that pure facts or statistics in themselves have any normative value. To assert this would be a great blunder, since to do so would be *a fortiori* to attribute an even more massive authority to the much more massive factual dimension of the existing Church order. The official Church order has, however, to justify itself with regard to varying experiences of Christians in respect of that Church order in history. In the same way, the new alternative and critical forms of praxis in the Church and the Church's office also have to justify themselves with regard to our historical experiences. A simple alternative—something that is new for its own sake—is meaningless. A particular praxis in the Christian community, whether it is new or old, is only authoritative if it contains the Christian *logos*, that is, the apostolicity of the Christian community. As Paul said, everything is permitted, but not everything leads to salvation.

Accounts of new alternative forms of praxis in the Church are historically always connected to memories and experiences of what has failed, sometimes absurdly, in the valid system and of the obstacles raised by that system. It is quite legitimate to take as one's point of departure when judging the authority of an alternative praxis in the Church such factors as our present-day experience of our own existence, the demands made by contemporary man and human rights. This is also the obvious way to proceed. I would personally prefer, in view of my experience of the toughness of any system, to take another and strategically more advantageous starting-point. I would therefore begin with what is accepted and defended by both parties in the Church from the point of view of the building up of the Christian community. By both parties here, I mean those who defend the official prevailing Church order and those who advocate an alternative critical praxis.

My point of departure, then, is the right of the Christian community to be able to do everything that is necessary to become a true community of Jesus and to extend that community. This right, both parties would agree, has to be exercised in union with and subject to the criticism of all the other Christian communities. This is a situation which can impose certain restrictions, as Vatican II pointed out. A variant of this starting-point would be the right of the Christian community to the Eucharist as the heart of the community. (The Second Vatican Council also stressed this aspect of the life of the community.) Another variant is the apostolic right of the community to leaders, a leader or a 'significant other person' who will clarify or give dynamic power to the fundamental values of the group or criticise the community.

The official Church also accepts these apostolic affirmations, but at the same time takes as its point of departure decisions that have already been made in the history of the Church (concerning, for example, the criteria for admission to the Church's office). These may in fact be an obstacle to this original right of the community to a leader when the world and the Church are placed in different circumstances. The present shortage of priests (which can be explained, at least partly, in the light of previously made decisions in the history of the Church) has led, for example, to all kinds of substitutes for the ministries of the Church. In addition to an authentic multiplicity of differentiated ministries (necessary in the situation in which Christian communities are placed today), an inauthentic multiplicity has also arisen, only because ordination or sacramental accreditation to and by the community has been withheld.

The difficulty confronting the image of the priest today can easily be seen if it is approached in this way, in the light of what is accepted by those who defend the existing Church order and by those who propose an alternative praxis. It should be quite clear to everyone that, in present circumstances, the celebration of the Eucharist is threatened, reduced to a banal level or even impeded. It is also evident from a great number of accounts of negative experiences of the 'service' priest's functioning within a sacral view of the Church's office that this image of the priest makes the Christian meaning of the community and the Eucharist in contemporary society ridiculous.

This is happening, moreover, at a time when there are, in many countries, very many men and women giving themselves wholeheartedly and sometimes for many years to pastoral work in their Christian community. It is only too obvious from the negative experiences that have been recorded that the existing Church order has become ossified as an ideology and is an obstacle to what it originally intended to achieve. The only reason for this almost insuperable difficulty in an unchanging Church order is the absence of celibate male priests. (And celibacy and male sex are not theological concepts.)

Very many Christians are unable to accept this situation and for them these negative experiences are an incentive to initiate an alternative praxis, without waiting for the existing system to change. This is also the reason why the phenomenon of alternative praxis, which occurs almost everywhere at present, has a diagnostic significance with regard to the symptoms of serious sickness in the existing system and can function as a criticism of the ideology underlying the traditional practices. Christians instinctively recognise that the New Testament datum of the priority of the community over office (and *a fortiori* over criteria for admission to that office which are not in themselves necessary) is clearly expressed in this kind of alternative praxis. It is also a sociological fact that existing laws in any society (including that of the Church) are seldom contested if they are inwardly convincing. In the case of the Church, such dis-

K

pensations are disputed by no one as long as their (Christian) *logos* or rationality is not doubted.

At present, however, we are witnessing within the Church throughout the world a wave of alternative praxis and this in itself is a clear indication that the existing order in the Church has lost its credibility and is in urgent need of revision. That order no longer has the power to convince many Christians and the result is a spontaneous and widespread appearance of the socio-psychological mechanism of the *non acceptatio legis*. If the Church intends, despite these signs, to maintain the existing order, it will only be able to do this now by authoritarian means (because there is a complete lack of conviction in the case of many of the Church's 'subjects'). To follow this course would only make the situation more precarious, because an authoritarian way of imposing Church order would go against the grain in modern man's experience of his own existence.

The third effect of this alternative praxis is that of dynamism, because many Christians are gradually coming to recognise that this praxis provides a new credibility structure and that they can identify themselves with it. This dynamism is not to be found in the pure fact of alternative praxis. The dynamic force comes from the fact that Christians see in this new praxis a modern form of apostolicity because of the presence in it of the Christian *logos*. Since the new praxis strikes them as convincing, it eventually acquires authority and the power to recruit others. What we cannot claim, however, is that this conviction, which is based on experience and inspires and determines the lives of many Christian communities and their office-bearers, does not possess an inherent Christian apostolicity even before it is recognised publicly by the official Church and that it will only acquire that apostolicity when it has been sanctioned by the Church. On the contrary, recognition is granted later, after it has become clear that the Christian *logos* is already present in it as a meaningful Christian possibility here and now.

As a theologian, I am bound to say that the alternative praxis of critical Christian communities that are inspired by Jesus as the Christ is, in the first place, both dogmatically and apostolically possible (although I cannot go into all the details here). It is, in my opinion, a legitimate Christian and apostolic possibility which is demanded by our present needs. To call communities 'heretical' and to say that they are already outside the Church (because of their alternative praxis) is, I believe, meaningless from the point of view of the Church. In the second place, given the existing canonical order of the Church, this alternative praxis is not even *contra* or against the order, but *praeter ordinem*, that is, it is not in accordance with the letter of the Church's order (it is *contra* that letter), but it is in accordance with what (in earlier situations) that Church order really wanted to safeguard.

It is obvious that a situation of this kind can never be pleasant for the representatives of the prevailing Church order, but they should listen to the accounts given by Christians of their negative experiences with the present order and be alert to the damage that they do to Christian communities, the Eucharist and the Church's office. If they do not, they may be seen as defending an established system rather than the Christian community and its Eucharistic heart. At a time when men have become very sensitive to the power structure underlying many systems, to cling persistently to the prevailing system when all kinds of experiments (some of them, of course, no doubt lacking in substance) are flourishing would cause pain to those who still love the Church.

Since alternative praxis of the kind described here is not *contra* or directly opposed to Church order, but only *praeter ordinem*, it can also be defended from the ethical point of view when the Church is placed in difficult circumstances. (We cannot, of course, pass any judgement here on subjective intentions.) When certain spokesmen of the official Church speak in this context of 'people who have placed themselves outside the Church', they are not only expressing themselves peevishly and in a way that is alien to the Church—they are also speaking in a way that is very redolent of what the Church has always called 'heresy'. Even the Second Vatican Council had trouble in defining the frontiers of membership of the Church. There are, of course, such frontiers. That is undeniable. But who would presume to define them? What is more, to speak in this way is posthumously to call earlier centuries of authentic Christian experience heretical and to condemn the New Testament search for the best pastoral possibilities.

I would at the same time like to say in this context that it would be equally out of keeping with the apostolic spirit to pursue alternative praxis in a triumphalistic way. It must always be a temporarily abnormal situation in the life of the churches. Personally—and I stress that this is no more than a very personal conviction—I believe that there ought to be some kind of strategy or 'economy' of conflicts. Where, for example, there is clearly no urgent need for an alternative praxis based on the pastoral requirements of the Christian community or communities, there is also no need to put everything that is 'apostolically' or dogmatically possible into practice. If this is done, there is always a danger that, in critical communities, the community is subordinated to the problem of office and adapted on the basis of the office-bearers' own problems concerned with the crisis of identity.

We should also not make the alternative forms of praxis into a mystery. Our attitude should be governed by realism and sobriety. Renewal in the Church usually begins with illegal deviations and it rarely happens that attempts at renewal come from above. When this does happen, the attempts are sometimes dangerous. Vatican II is an example of both movements. In its Constitution on the Liturgy, the Council sanctioned, to a very great extent at least, the illegal liturgical practice that had arisen before the Council in France, Belgium and Germany. On the other hand, when the conciliar attempts at liturgical renewal were given a concrete form and expression after the Council—and were thus imposed from above—this renewal found many Christians quite unprepared, with the result that it met with resistance in many Church communities.

The objection is often raised that changes or alternative praxis are not justified in the Christian sense or from the point of view of the Church by the fact that they are different or new. This is basically correct, but it is incorrect in its implicit assumption, since the same can be said of the established Church order in changed circumstances. That order is not legitimated simply on the basis of the inertia of its own factual existence. It can also suspected of being in decline and therefore of being in fact an obstacle to the authentic life of Christians in the Church at a time when the image of man and the world is changing. What is venerable and old cannot take precedence over what is new simply because it is venerable and old.

It is possible that I shall be criticised for seeing the Church in an exclusively horizontal dimension, in other words, in accordance with the model of a social reality, and not as a charismatic datum from above. My reply to this criticism is to reject this dualism in the Church on the basis of the New Testament. Of course we should not speak exclusively in descriptive, empirical language about the Church. We must also speak in the language of faith about the Church as, for example, the 'community of Jesus', the 'body of the Lord' or the 'temple of the Holy Spirit'. In both kinds of language, however, we are speaking about the same reality.

The gnostics showed a strong tendency to divide the Church into a 'heavenly' part (that would nowadays be regarded as beyond the reach of sociologists) and an 'earthly' part (capable of every kind of evil). This same tendency is displayed in the criticism outlined in the preceding paragraph. The Second Vatican Council reacted strongly against the division of the Church into two parts; the Church, as a human 'society' and as the 'body of Christ', should not, it insisted, 'be considered as two realities', as 'the earthly Church' and the separate 'Church enriched with heavenly things' (*Lumen Gentium* I, 8).

The obstacle to the renewal of the Church's official ministries is based above all on this dualistic conception of the Church (a view that is often expressed in apparently Christian terms such as 'hierarchical'). The consequence of this is that (because of the shortage of priests) Christian lay people are allowed to be as actively employed as possible in the pastoral sphere, but are prevented from being sacramentally accredited to the

Church's office. We are, however, bound to ask whether this development in the direction of non-office-bearing or non-sacramentally confirmed pastoral workers (a development that can only be understood in the light of the historical impediments that have been imposed on the Church's office) is theologically sound. All that we can say with certainty is that it preserves the superseded sacral image of the priest.

Finally, I should point out that it would, in my opinion, be wrong to place all the blame for this on Rome. Leadership or authority can only be exercised meaningfully and appear in changed forms if both the people and their office-bearers (including the bishops) have reached a sufficient level of consciousness. It is not possible to ask the highest authority in a world Church to change the order prevailing in that Church if that change does not meet with the approval of the majority of Christian communities. To do this would probably mark the beginning of a massive schism, requiring an equally massive ecumenical operation twenty years later. We have been made wiser, let us hope, by our knowledge of previous divisions in the history of the Church.

For this reason, I regard the critical alternative communities as ferment in a universal process which Christain consciousness is being formed and therefore as a necessarily exceptional position within the one great union of the apostolic churches. They occupy a marginal position, continuously stimulating Christian consciousness, so that the great Church will be made ready to receive another Church order which is more suitable for the modern world and its pastoral needs and which will give a contemporary form in our own times to the apostolic character of the Christian community.

Translated by David Smith

Notes

1. Jerome *Dialogus contra Luciferianos* c. 21; *PL* 23, 175.

2. Some have been discussed elsewhere in this issue. See also F. Klostermann, ed. *Der Priestermangel und seine Konsequenzen* (Düsseldorf 1977).

3. I have not attempted to analyse the different structures of office in the New Testament here. For this the reader should consult the relevant exegetical works. All that I have done is to outline the spirit in which office in the Church is viewed in the New Testament.

4. 1 Cor. 12:28, where official ministries are mentioned together with all kinds of other, non-official ministries.

5. *PG* 104, 558; see also 104, 975-1218; 137, 406-410. See also P. Joannou

Discipline Générale Antique I-1 (Grottaferrata 1962) pp. 74-75; V. Fuchs *Die Ordinationstitel. Von seiner Entstehung bis auf Innozenz III* (Bonn 1930); C. Vogel 'Vacua manus impositi' in *Mélanges liturgiques* (B. Botte) (Louvain 1972) 511-524; J. Martin *Die Genese des Amtspriestertum in der frühen Kirche* (Freiburg 1972).

6. For the Jewish background to the Christian idea of *cheirotonia* as *cheirothesia* (laying on of hands), see K. Hruby 'La Notion d'ordination dans la tradition juive' *La Maison-Dieu* 102 (Paris 1970) 52-72; E. Lohse *Die Ordination im Spätjudentum und im Neuen Testament* (Göttingen 1951); A. Ehrhardt 'Jewish and Christian Ordination' *Journal of Ecclesiastical History* 5 (1954) 125-138.

7. Cyprian *Epist.* 4, 5; *PL* 50, 434. See also F. Nikolasch *Bischofswahl durch alle konkrete Vorschläge* (Grass and Cologne 1973); K. Ganzer *Papsttum und Bistumbesetzungen in der Zeit von Gregor IX bis Bonifaz VIII* (Cologne 1968), which describes the historical development leading to the break with the earlier Church order.

8. Leo Magnus *Ad Anast. PL* 54, 634. See also L. Mortari *Consecrazione episcopale e collegialità* (Florence 1969); H. Dombois *Das Recht der Gnade* (Witten 1961); R. Kottje 'The Selection of Church Officials' *Concilium* 63 (1971) 117-126; H. M. Legrand 'Theology and the Election of Bishops' in the Early Church' *Concilium* 77 (1972) 31-42.

9. Paulinus *Epist. I ad Severum* c. 10: *CSEL* 29, 9.

10. Isidore *De ecclesiasticis officiis* II, 3: *PL* 83, 779.

11. There has been some discussion of the so-called *chorepiscopi* or bishops of country districts, but this situation confirms the principle of the early *titulus Ecclesiae*; see A. Bergère *Etudes historiques sur les chorévêques* (Paris 1925); T. Gottlob *Der abendländische Chorepiskopat* (Amsterdam 1963).

12. C. Vogel 'Laica communione contentus. Le retour du presbytre au rang des laics' *Recherches de Science Religieuse* 47 (1973) 56-122.

13. There are traces of the transition from *cheirotonia* (accreditation or *ordinatio* by means of an official acceptance on the part of the community) to a liturgical *cheirothesia* (or impostion of hands) in 1 Tim. 5:22; 2 Tim. 1:6; see also 1 Tim. 4:14.

14. B. Botte *La Tradition apostolique de saint Hippolyte, Sources chrétiennes* 11 bis (Paris 1963) (= *Liturgiewissenschaftliche Quellen und Forschungen* 39 ed. B. Botte [Münster 1963]); B. Botte 'L'Ordination de l'évêque' *La Maison-Dieu* 98 (Paris 1969) 113-126, and *Etudes sur le sacrement de l'ordre* (Paris 1957) 13-35; A. Rose 'La Prière de consécration par l'ordination épiscopale' *La Maison-Dieu* 98 (Paris 1969) 127-142; C. Vogel 'L'Imposition des mains dans les rites d'ordination en Orient et en Occident' *La Maison-Dieu* 102 (Paris 1970) 57-72; *ibid.* Le Ministère charismatique de l'eucharistie' *Studia Anselmiana* 61 (Rome 1973) 181-209; J. Lécuyer 'Episcopat et presbytérat dans les écrits d'Hippolyte de Rome' *Recherches de Science Religieuse* 41 (1953) 30-50; H. J. Schulz 'Das liturgisch sakramental übertragene Hirtenamt in seiner eucharistischen Selbstverwirklichung nach dem Zeugnis der liturgischen Überlieferung' in P. Bläser et al. *Amt und Eucharistie* (Paderborn 1973) pp. 208-255; *ibid.* Die Grundstruktur des kirchlichen Amtes im Spiegel der Eucharistiefeier und der

Ordinationsliturgie des römischen und des Byzantinischen Ritus' *Catholica* 29 (1975) 325-340; H.-M. Legrand 'Theology and the Election of Bishops', cited in note 8; J. H. Hanssens 'Les Oraisons sacramentelles des ordinations orientales' *Orient. Christ. Periodica* 18 (1952) 297-318; V. Brockhaus *Charisma und Amt* (Wuppertal 1962) pp. 674-676; V. Fuchs *Der Ordinationstitel*, cited in note 5.

15. Hippolytus *Traditio Apostolica* 2, 7 and 8.

16. Y. Congar 'Ordinations *invitus*, *coactus*, de l'Eglise antique au canon 214' *Revue des Sciences Philosophiques et Théologiques* 50 (1966) 169-197.

17. Hippolytus *Traditio*, 9.

18. *ibid.* 11 and 13; see also 15 and 19. In the *Constitutiones Apostolorum* 8, 21, 2 and 8, 22, 2, which are dependent on the *Traditio Apostolica* and appeared at the end of the fourth century A.D., hands are also laid on sub-deacons and lectors, in other words, the process of clericalisation was continued.

19. B. Botte *La Tradition apostolique*, cited in note 14, pp. 28-29. Botte denies that the confession made by suffering or *martyrium* replaced ordination. See also C. Vogel 'L'Imposition des mains', in the article cited in note 14. These scholars are right in that those who bore witness to faith were not automatically 'leaders' (even though they already possessed the charisma of the Spirit). A *receptio Ecclesiae* (and therefore *cheirotonia*, but without *cheirothesia*) continued to be required. See M. Lods *Confesseurs et Martyrs, successeurs des prophètes dans l'Eglise des trois premiers siècles* (Paris and Neuchâtel 1950); D. van Damme 'Martus, Christianos' *Freiburger Zeitschrift für Philosophie und Theologie* 23 (1976) 186-303.

20. See V. Saxer *Vie liturgique et quotidienne à Carthage vers le milieu du IIe siècle* (Rome 1969) pp. 194-202; A. Jansen *Kultur und Sprache. Zur Geschichte der alten Kirche im Spiegel der Sprachentwicklung von Tertullian bis Cyprian* (Nijmegen 1938).

21. *Sacerdos vice Christi vere fungitur* (Cyprian *Litt.* 63; PL 4, 386). See B. D. Marliangeas *Clés pour une théologie du ministère* (Paris 1979) p. 47.

22. Augustine *Contra Ep. Parmeniani* II, 8, 15 and 16: *CESL* 51, 1908 (*PL* 43, 49-50).

23. See P. M. Gy 'La Théologie des prières anciennes pour l'ordination des évêques et des prêtres' *Revue des Sciences philosophiques et théologiques* 58 (1974) 599-617.

24. B. Botte 'Secundi meriti munus' *Questions liturgiques et paroissiales* 21 (1936) 84-88.

25. This is what J. Blank claims in *Das Recht der Gemeinde auf Eucharistie. Die bedrohte Einheit von Wort und Sakrament* (Trier 1978) pp. 8-29. This view has to be given a little more light and shade (see further).

26. See K. Hruby 'La "Birkat ha-mazon"' *Mélanges Liturgiques* (Louvain 1972) 205-222; L. Finkenstein 'The Birkat ha-mazon' *Jewish Quarterly Review* 19 (1928-1929) 211-262; T. Talley 'De la "Berakah" à l'Eucharistie' *La Maison-Dieu* 125 (1974) 199-219.

27. See J. Audet *La Didachè* (Paris 1958).

28. Tertullian *De Corona* 3. See also Justin 1 *Apol.* 65, 3 and 67, 5. See also A. Quacquarelli 'L'epiteto sacerdote (hieres) ai crestiani in Giustino Martire, Dial. 116, 3' *Vetera Christianorum* 7 (1971); C. Vogel 'Le Ministère charismatique de

l'eucharistie' *Ministères et célébration de l'Eucharistie* pp. 198-204; M. Bévenot 'Tertullian's Thoughts about the Christian Priesthood' *Corona Gratiarum*, Part 1 (Bruges 1975).

29. See Ignatius of Antioch *Ad Smyrn.*, 8, 1-2. See also M. Jourgon 'La Présidence de l'eucharistie chez Ignace d'Antioche' *Lumière et Vie* 16 (1967) 26-32; R. Padberg 'Das Amtsverständnis der Ignatiusbriefe' *Theologie und Glaube* 62 (1972) 47-54; H.-M. Legrand 'La Présidence de l'eucharistie selon la tradition ancienne' *Spiritus* 18 (1977) 409-431.

30. Cyprian *Epist.* 45.

31. Cyprian *Litt.* 69, 9, 3; 72, 2, 1; *De unitate Ecclesiae* 17.

32. This is a tradition that was valid both in the East and in the West. See, for example, Jerome *Epist.* 15, 2; Innocent I *Epist.* 24, 3; Leo Magnus *Epist.* 80, 2; Pelagius I *Epist.* 24, 14; Aphraetes *Dem.* 12 de Paschate 9; *Decret. Gratiani* II, c. 1, q. 1, c. 73 and 78; Peter Lombard *Sententiae* IV, d. 13.

33. This can be found in *Vita Zephyrini* 2 (ed. L. Duchesne I, pp. 139-40).

34. See D. Droste *'Celebrare' in der römischen Liturgiesprache* (Munich 1963), especially pp. 73-80; R. Schultze *Die Messe als Opfer der Kirche* (Münster 1959); R. Raes 'La Concélébration eucharistique dans les rites orientaux' *La Maison-Dieu* 35 (1953) 24-47; R. Berger *Die Wendung 'offerre pro' in der römischen Liturgie* (Münster 1965); Y. Congar 'L'Ecclesia ou communauté chrétienne sujet intégral de l'action liturgique' *La liturgie d'après Vatican II* (Paris 1967) pp. 241-282; E. Dekkers 'La Concélébration, tradition ou nouveauté?' *Mélanges Liturgiques* (Louvain 1972) 99-120; B. Botte 'Note historique sur la concélébration dans l'Eglise ancienne' *La Maison-Dieu* 35 (1953) 9-23.

35. See, for an apparent exception in the Gelasian Sacramentary, Droste, in the work cited in note 34 at p. 80.

36. At the end of the eleventh century, Guerricus of Igny wrote: 'The priest does not consecrate alone and he does not sacrifice alone. The whole assembly of believers consecrates and offers together with him' (*Sermo* 5: *PL* 185, 57).

37. See especially E. Dekkers in the article cited in note 34, 110-112; R. Berger, in the article cited in the same note, 246; R. Schultze in the article cited in the same note, 188.

38. 1 Clem, 44, 4-6. See also M. Jourgon 'Remarques sur le vocabulaire sacerdotal de la Prima Clementis' *Epektasis* (In honour of Card. Daniélou) (Paris 1972) p. 109; J. Blond *L'Eucharistie des premiers chrétiens* (Paris 1948) pp. 38-39.

39. See note 29 above.

40. Tertullian *De Exhort. Cast.*, 7, 3; see also *De praescriptione* 41, 5-8; see also G. Otranto 'Nonne et laici sacerdotes sumus? (Exhort. Cast. 7, 3)' *Vetera Christianorum* 8 (1971) 24-47.

41. See G. Otranto 'Il sacerdozio commune dei fideli nei reflessi della 1 Petr. 3, 9' *Vetera Christianorum* 7 (1970) 225-246. See also J. Delorme 'Sacerdoce du Christ et ministère (à propos de Jean 17)' *Recherches de Science Religieuse* 62 (1974) 199-219; J. H. Elliot *The Elect and the Holy. An Exegetical Examination of 1 Peter 2, 4-10* (Leiden 1966). It should be noted that the term 'priestly people of God' does not have a cultic significance. It points to the election of the Christian community.

42. Augustine *Litt.* 3, 8: *CSEL* 34, 655.

43. See note 40 above.

44. *Decretum Gratiani* I, d. 70, c.l: ed. Friedberg, I p. 254; see also Hugh of Saint Victor *De Sacramentis*, II, p. 3, c. 2: *PL* 176, 421.

45. Mansi XXII, 220; see also R. Foreville *Latran I, II, III et Latran IV* (Paris 1965).

46. Denzinger and Schönmetzer 1764 and 1776.

47. Fourth Lateran Council, Denzinger and Schönmetzer 802.

48. See Denzinger and Schönmetzer 825. See also, among others, E. Dassmann *Charakter indelebilis. Anpassung oder Verlegenheit* (Cologne 1973); H.-M. Legrand 'The "Indelible" Character and the Theology of Ministry' *Concilium* 74 (1972) 54-62; P. Fransen 'Wording en strekking van de canon over het merkteken in Trente' *Bijdragen* 32 (1972) 2-34. See also note 49 below.

49. E. Schillebeeckx *Sacramentele heilseconomie* (Antwerp and Bilthoven 1952) pp. 501-536.

50. Denzinger and Schönmetzer 781 and 825.

51. See P. Fransen, in the article cited in note 48, and E. Schillebeeckx, in the workd cited in note 49.

52. This ontologisation of the character in the modern era and especially in the spirituality of the priesthood can be seen, for example, in the theory suggested by J. Galot, who made the character the foundation of priestly celibacy; see his 'Sacerdoce et célibat' *Nouvelle Revue Théologique* 86 (1964) 119-124.

53. *Summa Theologiae* 3a. q. 63, a. 5. This also applied to the characters of baptism and confirmation, each in its own specific way.

54. R. J. Cox *A Study of the Juridic Status of Laymen in the Writings of the Medieval Canonists* (Washington 1959); L. Hödl *Die Geschichte der scholastischen Literatur und der Theologie der Schlüsselgewalt* (Münster 1960); W. Plöchl *Geschichte des Kirchenrechtes* (Vienna, 2nd. edn. 1960) I p. 224ff; K. J. Becker *Wesen und Vollmachten des Priestertums nach dem Lehramt* (Freiburg 1970) pp. 113-121; M. van de Kerckhove 'La Notion de jurisdiction dans la doctrine des Décrétistes et des premiers Décrétalistes, de Gratian (1140) à Bernard de Bottone' *Etudes Franciscaines* 49 (1937) 420-455; P. Krämer *Dienst und Vollmacht in der Kirche. Eine rechtstheologische Untersuchung zur Sacra Potestas-Lehre des II. Vatikanischen Konzils* (Trier 1973); Y. Congar *Sainte Eglise* (Paris 1963) pp. 203-238; *ibid.* 'R. Sohm nous interroge encore' *Revue des Sciences Philosophiques et Théologiques* 57 (1973) 263-294; J. Ratzinger 'Opfer, Sakrament und Priestertum in der Entwicklung der Kirch' *Catholica* 26 (1972) 108-125; *ibid. Das neue Volk Gottes* (Düsseldorf 2nd. edn. 1970) pp. 75-245.

55. *Speculum Doctrinale* VIII, 34. See G. de Lagarde *La Naissance de l'esprit laique au déclin du Moyen-Age* I (Louvain and Paris 1956).

56. From the Carolingian period onwards, this tendency towards privatisation is noticeable and the earlier idea of *tota aetas concelebrat* became a mere *in voto* by the whole people; see, for example, Innocent III *De sacro altaris mysterio* III, 6: *PL* 217, 845.

57. See, for example, O. Nussbaum *Kloster, Priestermönch und Privatmesse* (Bonn 1961); A. Häussling *Mönchkonvent und Eucharistiefeier* (Münster 1973).

58. M. de Lubac *Corpus Mysticum. L'eucharistie et l'Eglise au Moyen-âge*

(Paris 2nd. edn., 1949); Y. Congar *L'Église de saint Augustin à l'époque moderne* (Paris 1970) pp. 167-173 (= *Handbuch der Dogmengeschichte*, III-3c [Freiburg 1971] pp. 105-108).

59. Expressing the view of all medieval theologians, Thomas said: *Sacramentum ordinis ordinatur ad eucharistiae consecrationem* (*Summa Theologia* 3a q. 65, a. 3).

60. Denzinger and Schönmetzer 802. A more precise formula was suggested in 1957 in a *Responsum Sancti Officii*: 'Ex institutione Christi ille solus valide celebrat qui verba consecratoria pronunciat'. (*Acta Apostolicae Sedis* 49 (1957) 370).

61. See J. P. Massaut *Josse Clichtove. L'humanisme et la réforme du clergé* 2 volumes (Paris 1969); also the critical discussion by G. Chantraine 'J. Clichtove: témoin théologique de l'humanisme parisien' *Revue d'Histoire Ecclésiastique* 66 (1971) 507-528. See also H. Jedin 'Das Leitbild des Priesters nach dem Tridentinum und dem Vatikanum II' *Theologie und Glaube* 60 (1970) 102-124.

62. *Summa Theologiae*, 2a, 2ae, q. 88, a. 11.

63. See A. Rohrbasser, ed. *Sacerdotis imago. Päpstliche Dokumente über das Priestertum von Pius X bis Johannes XXIII* (Freiburg 1962). For a historical survey of these tendencies, see E. Schillebeeckx, 'Creatieve terugblik als inspiratie voor het ambt in de toekomst'. *Tijdschrift voor Theologie* 3 (1979) 266-293.

64. A. Acerbi *Due ecclesiologie. Ecclesiologia giuridice ed ecclesiologie di communione nella 'Lumen Gentium'* (Bologna 1975); P. J. Cordes *Sendung und Dienst* (Frankfurt 1972); P. Krämer *Dienst und Vollmacht in der Kirche* (Trier 1973); Y. Congar 'Préface' in B. D. Marliangeas *Clés pour une théologie du ministère* (Paris 1978) pp. 5-14. See also note 54 above.

65. Isa. 24. 2; Hos. 4. 9.

66. 1 Clem. 40. 4-5.

67. *Traditio Apostolica* 3. Hippolytus here insists that the bishop has the task of coordinating the *klerio*, in other words, the different ministries.

68. An interpolation, taken from one of Pius XII's encyclical letters, will be found in *Lumen Gentium*, 10. According to this insertion, the priesthood of all believers differs essentially from the official priesthood (*essentia et non tantum gradu differunt*). In the light of the whole Church's tradition, this must be interpreted as an affirmation of the specific nature of this Church office, not an insistence on a difference in status.

69. See, for example, Bonaventure *In IV Sent*. d. 24, p. 1, a. 2, q. 2; Thomas Aquinas *In IV Sent*., d. 24, q. 1, a. 1, ad 1.

70. For the origin of the term *ordo*, see P. van Beneden *Aux Origines d'une terminologie sacramentelle: ordo, ordinare, ordinatio dans la littérature latine avant 313* (Louvain 1974); B. Kübler 'Ordo' in Pauly and Wissowa *Realenzyklopädie* XVIII-1 (Stuttgart 1939) pp. 930-934; T. Klauser *Der Ursprung der bischöflichen Insignien und Ehrenrechte* 2nd. edn. (Krefeld 1953).

71. B. D. Dupuy 'Theologie der kirchlichen Ämter' in J. Feiner and M. Löhrer, eds. *Das Heilsgeschehen in der Gemeinde, Mysterium Salutis* IV-s (Einsiedeln 1973) pp. 488-525, especially p. 495.

72. J. D. Zizioulas 'Ordination et communion'. *Istina* 16 (1971) 5-12, and H.

Vorgrimler, ed. *Amt und Ordination in ökumenischen Sicht* (Freiburg 1973) pp. 72-113.

73. This information is given in *De vita S. Gregorii Thaumaturgi: PG* 46, 909.

74. L. Hertling 'Communio und Primat' *Una Sancta* 17 (1962) 91-95; W. de Vries *Rom und die Patriarchate des Ostens* (Freiburg and Munich 1963); N. Afanassieff *et al. La primauté de Pierre dans l'Eglise Orthodoxe* (Neuchâtel 1960); A. Brandenburg and H. J. Urban, eds. *Petrus und Papst* (Münster 1977); H. J. Mund, ed. *Das Petrusamt in der gegenwärtigen theologischen Diskussion* (Paderborn 1976); K. J. Ohlig *Bracht die Kirche einen Papst?* (Mainz and Düsseldorf 1973); J. Ratzinger, ed. *Zum Wesen und Auftrag des Petrusamt* (Düsseldorf 1978).

75. *Lumen Gentium* 23 and 26; *Christus Dominus* 11; *Sacrosanctum Concilium passim.* See also H. Marot 'Note sur l'espression "episcopus catholicae Ecclesiae"' *Irenikon* 37 (1964) 221-226.

76. H.-M. Legrand *Unam Sanctam* 74 pp. 105-121 and 'The Revaluation of Local Churches: Some Theological Implications' *Concilium* 71 (1972) 53-64; L. Ott *Le sacrement de l'ordre* (Paris 1971), especially pp. 42-44.

77. Denzinger and Schönmetzer, 1776.

78. *Lumen Gentium* 28.

Contributors

MONIQUE BRULIN, born in 1943, holds degrees in economics (Aix-en-Provence) and theology (Institut Catholique de Paris). She works for the Centre National de Pastorale Liturgique in Paris, and has written on Penance and on Sunday Assemblies.

KARL DERKSEN, OP, was born at Emmerich, Holland, in 1937, became a Dominican and studied philosophy and theology at Zwolle, Nijmegen and Münster. He is a lecturer in western religions at the Humanist Formation Centre at Culemborg, a theological collaborator of the movement of grass-roots communities and radical parishes in Holland and editor of various reviews. Within the Dutch province of the Dominican Order he is responsible for study and formation. He has published articles on monastic life, Christians for Socialism, solidarity, and the movement of grass-roots communities and radical parishes.

SEVERINO DIANICH was born in Fiume in 1934 and studied at Pisa and then in Rome, where he took a degree on theology at the Gregorian. Ordained in 1958, he has been parish priest of a small town near Pisa since 1966. He is vice-president of the Italian Theological Institute and a member of the 'Dogma' editorial board of *Concilium*. He was co-editor of the *Nuovo Dizionario di Teologia* (Ed. Paoline, 1977) and has published several studies on the meaning of the priesthood and the mission of the Church, of which the most recent is *Il prete: a che serve? Saggio di teologia del ministero ordinato* (Rome 1978).

GIOVANNI FRANZONI, who was born in 1928, was a Benedictine monk from 1950-1974. Formerly Abbot of St Paul's outside the Walls in Rome, he resigned after he got into trouble with the Curia in 1973 and was suspended as a result of his stand at the time of the divorce referendum in 1974. Reduced to the lay state in 1975, today he is a member of the basic community of S. Paolo and of the editorial staff of the weekly *Com/Nuovi Tempi*. Notable among his publications are: *La terra è di Dio*, a pastoral letter written on the occasion of the proclamation of the Holy Year (Com/Nuovi Tempi); *Il mio regno non e di questo mondo* (Com/Nuooi Tempi); *Le Comunita di Base* (Genoa); *Tra le gente* (Com/Nuovi Tempi); *Il posto della fede* (Coines).

NORBERT GREINACHER was born in 1931 at Freiburg-im-Breisgau, Germany. He was ordained to the priesthood in 1956. He is professor of pastoral theology at the University of Tübingen. Among his published works are: *Die Kirche in der städtischen Gesellschaft* (Mainz 1966); *Soziologie der Pfarrei* (Freiburg-im-Breisgau 1955); (with W. Menges) *Zugehörigkeit zur Kirche* (Mainz 1964); *2000 Briefe an die Synode* (Mainz 1971); *Angst in der Kirche verstehen und überwinden* (Mainz 1972); *Christliche Rechtfertigung—Gesellschaftliche Gerechtigkeit* (Zürich 1973); (with R. Zerfass) *Einführung in die Praktische Theologie* (Munich 1976); (with F. Klostermann) *Vor einen neuen politischen Katholizismus?* (Frankfurt 1978).

JAN KERKHOFS, SJ, was born in 1924 and became a Jesuit. He studied in Louvain, Münster and Oxford, and obtained a licentiate in philosophy and theology and a doctorate in sociology. He now teaches pastoral sociology at the theological faculty of Louvain University and is Secretary-General of the international study and information centre Pro Mundi Vita in Brussels. He is also ecclesiastical adviser to Uniapac-international.

JOSEPH KOMONCHAK, was born in Nyack (New York) in 1939 and ordained in 1963. After serving in a parish for three years, he taught systematic theology at St Joseph's Seminary for ten years. Since 1977, he has been an associate professor in the Department of Religion and Religious Education at the Catholic University of America, Washington, D.C. He has written articles on such topics as the contraception debate, liberation theology and the ordination of women, in various theological journals.

JOAN LLOPIS, was born in Barcelona in 1932. He studied at the University of Salamanca, the Gregorian University and the Liturgical Institute of San Anselmo in Rome. He has been professor of liturgy in the University of Salamanca and in the Faculty of Theology at Barcelona. He is a founder member of the Centro de Pastoral Litúrgica in Barcelona, and a member of the editorial committee of the liturgical section of *Concilium*. He has published a number of works on liturgy.

FRITZ LOBINGER, was born in 1929 in Passau, Germany, and ordained diocesan priest of Regensburg in 1955. Between 1956-1969 he was a Fidei Donum missionary in a Xhosa parish, Aliwal diocese, S. Africa. In 1971 he did a doctoral thesis on the transitory role of the pastor-catechist in Münster. Between 1971-1973 he was director of the Catechist School Lumko. Since 1974 he has been directing the Pastoral Department of Lumko Missiological Institute of the Southern African Bishops' Conference, being mainly engaged in re-orientation courses for priests and pastoral workers and as editor of the series 'Training for Community Ministries'.

EDWARD SCHILLEBEECKX, OP, was born at Antwerp (Belgium) in 1914 and was ordained in 1941. He studied at Louvain, Le Saulchoir, the Ecole des Hautes Etudes and the Sorbonne (Paris). He became a doctor of theology in 1951 and *magister* in 1959. Since 1958, he has been teaching dogmatic theology and hermeneutics at the University of Nijmegen (Netherlands). He is the editor-in-chief of the *Tijdschrift voor Theologie*. In addition to very many articles, he has written a number of books, including: *Christ the Sacrament of the Encounter with God* (New York 1963), *Revelation and Theology* (London 1968), *God and Man* (New York 1969), *World and Church* (New York 1971), *The Understanding of Faith* (London and New York 1974), *Jesus, An Experiment in Christology* (New York 1979), *Gerechtigheid en liefde* (Bloemendaal 1977) and many others.

HANS-JÜRGEN VOGELS, was born in Berlin in 1933 and ordained priest in Cologne in 1959. Since 1967 he has been one of the team at the Albertus-Magnus-Institut in Bonn working on an edition of the works of Albert the Great. He gained his doctorate in 1975 with a thesis on the credal article 'descended into hell' and has written a book on priestly celibacy *Pflichtzölibat. Eine kritische Untersuchung* (Munich 1978).

HANS WALDENFELS, SJ, was born in Essen/Ruhr (Germany) in 1931. A Jesuit, he was ordained priest in Tokyo in 1963. He has studied philosophy, theology, comparative religion and philosophy of religion at Pullach bei München, Tokyo, Kyoto, Rome and Münster. He received his doctorate in theology at Würzburg and is professor of fundamental theology, non-Christian religions and philosophy of religion at the University of Bonn. Among other things he has published: *Offenbarung* (Munich 1969), *Glauken hat Zukunft* (Freiburg 1970), *Meditation—Ost und West* (Einsiedeln 1975), *Absolutes Nichts* (Freiburg 1976, 1978).

DECLARATION OF CONCILIUM

We, directors of the international review of theology *Concilium,* do not see any well-founded reason not to consider our colleague Hans Küng as a Catholic theologian.

We shall, therefore, press to have the judgment reconsidered.

In addition we ask with emphasis that the ecclesiastical procedure in religious matters will respect the commonly established rules of human rights.

Professor Jürgen Moltman of Tübingen has indicated that he wishes to be associated with the fuller statement of the editorial directors published in our issue No. 10 1979.